Things I Will Tell You When I Am Dead

Things I Will Tell You
When I Am Dead

Kathleen Whelan

First Edition

Hidden Brook Press
www.HiddenBrookPress.com
writers@HiddenBrookPress.com

Copyright © 2017 Hidden Brook Press
Copyright © 2017 Kathleen Whelan

All rights for story and characters revert to the author. All rights for book, layout and design remain with Hidden Brook Press. No part of this book may be reproduced except by a reviewer who may quote brief passages in a review. The use of any part of this publication reproduced, transmitted in any form or by any means, electronic, mechanical, photocopied, recorded or otherwise stored in a retrieval system without prior written consent of the publisher is an infringement of the copyright law.

This book is a work of fiction. Names, characters, places and events are either products of the author's imagination or are employed fictitiously. Any resemblance to actual events, locales or persons, living or dead, is entirely coincidental.

Things I Will Tell You When I Am Dead
by Kathleen Whelan

Editor – Elizabeth Philips
Cover Photograph – David Bateman
Cover Design – David Bateman
Layout and Design – Richard M. Grove

Typeset in Garamond
Printed and bound in USA
Distributed in USA by Ingram,
in Canada by Hidden Brook Distribution

Library and Archives Canada Cataloguing in Publication

Whelan, Kathleen, 1950-, author
    Things I will tell you when I am dead / Kathleen Whelan.
-- First edition.

Short stories.
ISBN 978-1-927725-25-2 (softcover)

        I. Title.

PS8645.H445T55 2017   C813'.6   C2017-900433-6

For Sara,
Sabrina
&
Jackie B.

Foreword by, Mary W. Walters

In "Energy," the opening story of this wonderfully funny, dark and moving collection of short fiction, Frances Breen – still barely able to absorb the shocking news that her husband of less than a year has just been killed in a hydrogen explosion at the nuclear plant where he works – must also absorb the words of a ghost named Augustine (yes. Like the saint) about the nature of her late husband's relationship with Frances's twin sister, who is now a nun.

This capsule setup barely suggests the range of characters and plot twists both real and spectral that press against the boundaries of the first story in Kathleen Whelan's debut collection of short stories. As "Energy" unfolds, it becomes clear why Frances's husband called her "a force to be reckoned with": it may be the early 1950s, but this is no typical 1950s homemaker. Her physical and emotional responses to her husband's death ("She took off her pink silk taffeta gown and climbed up onto the coffin. She wore no underwear"), and her resolutions for the future for her infant daughter ("Jack, you wanted Mona to someday drive a team of Norwegian ponies. With a straight back, a firm hand, and wearing handcrafted boots, she'll win first prize at the Sheenboro Fair") reveal a determined, self-reliant woman who is willing to accommodate the extraordinary while also firmly steering the bark of her own destiny.

Kathleen Whelan, too, is a "force to be reckoned with" – both as writer, and as a person.

I met Kathleen at a writers' colony in Saskatchewan about a decade ago. We knew immediately that we were kindred spirits: we were both dragging a lot of difficult and painful baggage into futures that we had determined would be better than our pasts, ones in which we could invest our hopes because above all, we knew that we were writers. When I moved to Toronto a few years later, it was Kathleen (who seemed to know everyone in the literary, dramatic and musical firmaments) who showed me around and helped make me feel at ease in the big city. In the years since, amid the vicissitudes of life – family crises, illnesses, the need to earn a living, winter – we have sustained one another in the way that only writer friends can do: by recognizing, understanding and reaffirming the creative imperative in one another.

Kathleen's life has had more than its share of tragedy and loss. Her own father died in a nuclear accident when she was a baby, and she lost her cherished niece Sabrina to a peanut allergy when Sabrina was only 13 (a death which, thanks to the efforts of Sabrina's mom, Sara, and Kathleen herself, ultimately lead to the introduction of anaphylaxis policies in schools across Canada and the U.S., including the enactment of Sabrina's Law in Ontario in 2005).

Since I have met Kathleen, I have admired the strength and courage with which she has faced other unimaginable challenges, including the deaths of two close friends. Rather than being diminished by these and other adversities she has faced, they seem to have strengthened her, and in that mysterious hopper called "the muse" they have formed some of the fodder for her fiction.

It is a joy for me to watch Kathleen launch this, her first book. The joy is in part for Kathleen, who at last will be able to hold a volume of her own writing in her hands, after having been such a constant, enthusiastic supporter of the artistic creations (prose and poetry, drama, music, performance and visual art) of so many of her friends. But my joy is also for readers, who will now have a chance to "hear" Kathleen's distinctive voice. Her writing reflects her nature: it is open, direct, honest, and funny. Her fictional characters, like their author, look at reality with occasional disbelief and pain, but always with courage, and always with humour.

I am so tempted to tell you to open this book immediately and check out one particular story or another (like the one where a teenaged girl runs into Prince Andrew on the ski slopes, or the one where an alcoholic, almost at her bottom, experiences a miracle in Greece, or the one about the woman who falls in love with a junkie while attempting to be born again into the Roman Catholic Church), but there are too many good ones. You will find them.

Kathleen is publishing her first full-length work of fiction later in life than most new writers do, but I have great confidence in her future as a writer, and I am already looking forward to her next book. In the meantime the powerful characters she has created in *Things I Will Tell You When I Am Dead* – many of whom share her dry wit, adventurous spirit, and Irish-Catholic heritage – have created a community in and about the imagined town of St. Columba in the Ottawa Valley that no reader will soon forget.

Enjoy.

Mary W. Walters
Toronto
2017

Contents

1. Energy – *p. 3*
2. Blueberry Pie – *p. 13*
3. A Prince is the Gift of Love – *p. 18*
3. Mock Duck – *p. 27*
4. Hope – *p. 35*
5. Irish Soda Bread – *p. 47*
6. Elvis was Dead – *p. 55*
7. Hush Puppies – *p. 60*
8. Bareback – *p. 65*
9. Geography – *p. 76*
10. Wonderland – *p. 83*
11. Smother the Others – *p. 89*
12. The Rock – *p. 100*
13. Angel Cake – *p. 105*

Acknowledgments – *p. 117*

Beneath Us

ice bound
silence is
a myth
I know
because I lay
one ear flush
to the surface
the effect
was like suction
and I heard
something
that flowed
and it flowed

Giovanni Malito
(1957-2003)

Energy

On January 30, 1950, Jack Breen was killed in a hydrogen explosion at a nuclear plant where he worked as a technician. The core of the reactor was destroyed and Jack's fantasy of making love to a nun dressed in a white habit floated unnoticed in twelve million gallons of radioactive water by the crew who cleaned up the spill.

That afternoon, Father Keon visited Frances Breen to tell her that her husband was dead.

Frances said, "There's mock duck in the oven for dinner, Mona is too young to crawl, and Jack is only thirty-two. He can't be dead."

"The president of the plant arranged for Harold Gribbon to identify the body. They will take care of the cost of the funeral. Be a good woman. You aren't the first to lose a husband. You have your baby Mona to sustain you. And the prayers of your twin to light the way."

"Tonight I'll be kissing Jack's cold lips," she said.

"Frances, Jack's face is a sorry sight. The coffin will be closed. The president wants to spare you the grief."

"Father Keon, I'm a trained nurse for heaven's sake."

"You have the baby to put you in mind of Jack."

"Yes. She has her father's feet."

Frances folded her arms and stared at the floor and waited for the priest to leave. She took Mona from her crib and said, "Today was your daddy's day off. I bundled you up and put you outside in your carriage to sleep. Fresh air is good for your lungs. Someone called in sick and your daddy went to work. Before he left for work, he brought you in from the cold. He said it was too windy outside and you might blow away."

Frances telephoned the Precious Blood Convent in Montreal where her twin sister lived.

She said to the Mother Superior, "I know that Sister St. Clare has taken a vow of silence. That I cannot speak to her. Please tell her that our Jack is dead and that he and I won't dance in the kitchen again. He won't be home for supper. Tell her that God did give me another cross to bear."

After she hung up the phone, Frances put Mona outside on the porch for some fresh air. She covered the carriage with a Kenwood blanket and said, "Mona you're named after your aunt. She now calls herself Sister St. Clare. I married your daddy and she gave herself to Jesus. She will say that this is my fault that Jack is gone."

Then Frances opened the oven and said, "Jack, why can't you stay put? This isn't funny. The promises you made are worth less than this dinner. You tricked me. You and the Lord have a cheap sense of humour."

Frances pressed a finger on her lower lip and said, "Shit."

The wake was held at the Gribbon Funeral Home. Frances stood in front of the coffin with Mona in her arms and imagined that next week a card would arrive from Deadwood, South Dakota that said, "Come and I'll have you on the table where Wild Bill played his last hand."

She giggled at the thought of Jack's foolish notion.

"Jack, you wanted Mona to someday drive a team of Norwegian ponies. With a straight back, a firm hand, and wearing handcrafted boots, she'll win first prize at the Sheenboro Fair."

The owner of the funeral home, Harold Gribbon, glanced at Frances with a concerned look.

"You're a good man, Harold, but I don't believe Jack is in that box. Not to worry. I know Jack can't hear me. Sign of the times, Harold. This is the first wake in our family to not be held in the living room out at the family farm. Our wedding breakfast was there on the day after Christmas. St. Stephen's Day. It was grand altogether. Here I am talking like my mother. Grand altogether and here we are two weeks before our first wedding anniversary."

Harold looked away and she tried to recall Jack's brown eyes.

Frances placed her hand on the coffin and said, "I won't have it. You're part of God's plan. The damn reason I'm still alive. Mona and I'll not move another step without you. Sister St. Clare told me when I had the ugly thing removed that God would give me another cross to bear. Jack, I was born with that tumour. It wasn't because I saw that plastic surgeon that this happened to you. But you know Sister St. Clare will say it is. I wish I could believe it. Then this would make sense. I'm a romantic fool and thought God saved me to be with you. And Mona. Harold's standing near. He must think I'm daffy talking to you this way."

A tall, lanky man appeared beside Frances. He said, "I've been on bloody Oiseaux Rock since the Napoleonic wars and long for the presence of a kindred spirit."

Frances thought of Oiseaux Rock and the first time she and Jack made love. She said, "Jack and I went there."

"It's a great arse you've on you. I watched the first time he had you."

Frances blushed.

She kissed Mona's feet and said, "Who the hell are you?"

"Augustine."

"No one is called Augustine. Except the saint, of course."

"Haven't heard a woman say my name since I was forced to come here and died of frostbite in a caboose shanty sleeping four to a bed. The British took the tallest lads from County Mayo. The bastards needed timber for their ships. They left the little ones alone. Knew they couldn't make the trip. The lads who tried to escape were strung up at Hangman's Hill back in the county. Irish slaves we were. Left us on the long shores without a hope of seeing our women or children again. They threw my frozen corpse at the foot of that fucking rock jutting out of the Ottawa River on December 13, 1816. A frozen Irish corpse left for the eagles."

Frances said, "I don't care. Women wept when Jack sang 'Your Cheating Heart.'

"I want my husband back."

Augustine said, "I warned him not to roam if he wanted to avoid an early grave. Perhaps he believed it was just drunken discourse with the moon and a ghost. Now he can wait for a glimpse of love on the rock. He talked to me when he was drunk. What better time to converse now that he is dead, too."

"Jack is really dead, then?"

"As dead as me. But not as long," he said.

"Baloney," she said.

"Jack took you on the rock. I watched. You and the Holy One. It's a sad day for you but many men are dead. You will make love again. Jack and I will not."

"Jack wouldn't give the likes of you the time day."

Harold put his arm around Frances and said, "Come and I'll make you a hot cup of tea. You're talking to the air."

Along the way to the coffee room, Frances said thank you to a few of the mourners.

"The Holy One?" she whispered.

Frances was angry at the Lord who teased her with Jack and left her to contend with the ghost and Harold's cup of tea. With Mona in her arms, Frances wondered what the Blessed Mother did to forget after they killed her son. Jack used to say the girls in tight skirts weren't as good a time as the ones in blue dresses. She thanked the Lord for the women in heaven and cursed her twin.

The reception area was empty and Frances sat on the couch while Harold made some tea. Frances felt as though she had a boil in her heart and she wanted desperately for it to burst. She shut her eyes and squinted tightly but not one tear could she expel. She heard a low humming sound and felt the presence of the ghost beside her. As a child she used to sit on only half her seat so that her guardian angel could share her chair. She wondered if she stretched out on the couch, would he lie on top of her.

Frances told herself to not play with evil thoughts. She wondered if Augustine could become Jack. Maybe he was the ghost of all the dead men that everyone was going on about.

Augustine and Father Keon insinuated that she was making much ado over nothing because so many men are dying on the job. Leaving their women with too much longing and not enough money. Father Keon thought the business of a being a widow would be her life. Running the house, caring for Mona and getting to mass. Showing up on Jack's anniversary every year to mourn his death. At least Augustine, who was dead, believed she would have another man. Maybe a dozen.

Frances reminded herself that she was alive because of God's grace. Years before, she survived a fire. She was in nursing school in Montreal. Frances slept soundly while the other students fled a burning residence. A friend noticed that Frances wasn't there, ran back in and shook her awake and helped Frances out to the street. The next morning, only a statue of the Blessed Mother stood unmarked amongst the ashes.

Frances laughed and said to Harold, "Jack is gone and suddenly I want to laugh myself silly."

"Only milk, isn't it, Frances?"

Frances said, "Jack knew. He knew this would happen. If only he hadn't come back and settled down."

Harold said, "Could've happened anywhere. Would you like a peanut butter cookie?"

Frances said, "I can't eat a bite. He knew this would happen. I didn't want to believe him. He dazzled me. On Victoria Day two years ago. Fireworks crackling in the sky and magic between us. He told me that he had never felt that way before. He kissed me when I still had a tumour on my lip. Jack held my face with his lovely hands and said, 'I don't want to fuck things up. I have to go.' Then he kissed me goodbye and left to find work in the west."

Frances could hear Augustine, but she could not see him. He sang softly:

Cold cold shanties of the Ottawa Valley
All lads who refused were hung
All the big Irishmen are in the Ottawa Valley
Timbering for British ships.

"Was the Holy One Sister St. Clare?" Frances asked.

Many men are dead, he hummed.

Harold said, "It's a tough call."

Frances said to Harold, "There's something eating away at me. A few months ago Sister St. Clare wrote to Jack. I hid the letter from him. I was afraid that in the calm he would stop loving me. And now he is silent too. She and I aren't identical, but we shared our mother's womb. You know that we are both nurses, and that she went overseas to work during the war. While she was in Europe, I did private duty in the homes of dying old men around here. On the men's ward they look forward to a good-looking dame to give them a bath. I was afraid to work on the floor because of my tumour."

"When St. Clare came back from overseas, she went out with Jack. Something else was calling her. That's what she said. Then she entered the Precious Blood. During the war she wrote that she desired to whip the soldiers as Jesus was whipped on the road to his crucifixion to distract them from the horrific possibilities awaiting them on the battlefield. I thought it an odd comment and wondered for the first time if she had a vocation. But I was shocked when she chose a cloistered order. She will never nurse again. I want her to break her vow of silence. I need to know if Jack will make her scream in her dreams."

Harold said, "He was a gentleman and would never do such a thing."

"Harold, turn your head for a bit. Mona needs some milk."

Harold stood, and with his back turned to Frances, made another pot of tea.

"After she took her final vows I went to Montreal and dropped by the Precious Blood to see her. A woman who looked like me dressed in white standing behind a white lattice partition met me with icy silence. Jack wasn't the only one she froze out. A few months later, Jack and I met at the Club Grill. He told me he was still in love with Sister St. Clare and then he took a shine to me."

Augustine said, "Jack had her out on the rock. I told him to take you both at the same time. But he didn't listen. Now he doesn't have either of you. Don't hate him."

Frances slipped her breast back in her dress and said, "Christ. In the summer let's row to the rock and put up a marker for a tall man from County Mayo. We need to remember him. And calm him down. Some other time I'll tell you more."

Harold nodded.

Frances took a cookie from the plate and said, "This is gorgeous."

"Thank you Augustine for telling me the truth."

Harold drove Frances home and said, "Who's Augustine?"

"A ghost from Oiseaux Rock. Don't say his name. He likes the sound of it. It's time for him to go back to the rock."

In bed with Mona, Frances wore Jack's coat over her nightie and placed his shoes on the empty pillow beside her. On Jack's night table there was an unread copy of *City of God*. She regretted that she would never care about St. Augustine.

Frances recalled Victoria Day and read the letters Jack wrote to her during the year he was away.

From Fort Smith he wrote, "The best is yet to come."

A post card from Dawson City read, "No one can replace you."

When Jack was in Banff, Frances went to Montreal to see a plastic surgeon to have the tumour removed. She wrote to her twin and told her nothing could be harder to bear.

By the time he arrived in Saskatoon, Jack was getting cold feet. "Frances, you're a force to be reckoned with and I fear marriage might steal our thunder."

The note from Winnipeg distressed Frances. "Today I saw an elk. Sex is amazing, but it is a fleeting thing. Last night I played in a bar. They say I'm as good as Hank Williams. Forgive me, Frances, but after our visit I'm going to Newfoundland."

A week later, they made love as though their lives depended on it. At the foot of Oiseaux Rock. They did not make love again until their honeymoon.

She blew gently over Mona's bald head and turned out the light.

Frances whispered to Mona, "Sweetheart, you were conceived at the Queen Elizabeth in Montreal. Your daddy had his feet on the ground. The day after you were born he took out an insurance policy for you. It matures when you turn sixty-five."

That night Frances dreamt that she and Mona lay on top of a white wooden bed waiting for Jack to return home. There was lavender scattered on lace pillow cases, linen sheets, pink crocheted quilt and hardwood floor. Jack walked into the room. He was dressed in the brown leather jacket that he bought in the Yukon and was carrying a battered overnight bag.

Jack smiled at Frances and said, "No one can replace you."

He kissed her breast, touched Mona's forehead and placed a tiny pair of roller skates on the pillow beside his daughter's head. There was a lipstick tube attached to one skate and to the other a hand-carved Norwegian pony.

Jack left a note that said, "I'm so lonesome, I could die."

Frances woke with a start, then fell into a delicious sleep lulled by the smell of lavender in the room.

On the last night of the wake, Frances left the baby in the care of a neighbour. She was the first to arrive at the funeral home and was alone with her husband. She stood and looked at Jack's picture and said, "The Mother Superior called. It will please you to know that Sister St. Clare wailed in Gaelic when she was told that you were dead. Our grandmother spoke a few of the old words. Leave it to St. Clare to remember them. Months ago, St. Clare wrote to you. I hid the letter."

"She wrote, 'Know I bathe in the blood of Jesus'."

"Maybe you'll understand, Jack, what the hell she meant. She must have been a cold fuck. My twin is a dangerous woman but I miss her. But it's your laugh I long to hear now. Last night you came to me in a dream."

She felt a tap on her shoulder. And she was relieved when she turned to see Harold.

He said, "Couldn't sleep last night. You've a right to some peace. There's not a mark on Jack's face. There is so much radioactivity in his pores that he'll light up the other graves at Saint Columba Cemetery. They had to tell me. It's a special protective coffin he's in. I am so sorry."

Frances cried and said, "Now I can imagine his brown eyes. Jack is dashing dead or alive. Harold, you're a good man."

"Don't cause trouble, Frances."

"Someday there will be trouble for the plant. But not for you."

Father Keon arrived to say the rosary with the Knights of Columbus. The priest said to Frances, "Wear a good suit to follow Jack up the aisle in the morning."

"Father Keon, get on with your Glory Be's. I'll do the right thing by my husband."

After the last decade of the beads, the priest left with the other mourners to go out for supper and booze. There was not a hint of Augustine in the room and Frances shuddered when she imagined him waiting on the rock. She said a prayer for him and the women he left behind.

Frances took the flowers off the top of the coffin and tried to open the lid. While she hummed "Cold Cold Heart," she took off her pink silk taffeta gown and climbed up onto the coffin. She wore no underwear. With her legs straddling the sides Frances put her hands on her breasts and closed her eyes.

Mona will wear good shoes.

She would tell Mona that her father gave up his life so that she could live. In its own time, the world would know the truth about how Jack died.

When Mona got older she would understand that her father died for no reason.

Frances lay the length of the coffin, took the red carnation from her hair and tucked it inside her vagina.

She thought, "Sex is not fleeting."

She removed the flower and ate a petal. Then she rubbed the flower gently around the head of the coffin.

She said, "I want you to go to heaven and for God's sake stay there. There's no need for you to be hanging about."

He used to do the supper dishes. On Saturdays he washed the kitchen floor. He told her she was a force to be reckoned with.

Frances held on to the sides of the coffin and wept while she kissed Jack goodbye.

"I am a force to be reckoned with," she said.

Blueberry Pie

The Nolan sisters lived a few blocks away from the one-bedroom apartment my mother and I shared. The sisters ran a beauty salon in the front room of their house. They also kept boarders in their home – men who, my mother claimed, sold children into the white slave trade.

Prowlers, carnies and boarders were men to stay away from. They might tie me to the mast of a tall ship. Being kidnapped and taken to the Ivory Coast sounded like a grand adventure, but the men my mother identified as dangerous seemed to all wear unpolished shoes and eat alone at the Club Grill.

While my mother had her hair done at the Nolans, I put pink curlers in my hair and watched for the smoky men who seemed poor and sad to me. In the beauty salon, there were detective magazines on the coffee table for customers to read, cigarettes in a silver container and an ashtray placed inside a tiny Michelin tire. My five-year-old body tingled when I looked at the drawings inside the publications the Nolans called "rags for dicks."

My mother laughed at the sisters' stories of going unescorted to the beverage room at the hotel. They told me the tire around the ashtray was from a leprechaun's tractor. My mother told them I spent hours looking for leprechauns under toadstools covered in pine needles. One of the sisters gave me a ceramic leprechaun. When I made my first communion they gave me the ashtray.

They would say to me, "Claire, someday you'll be a movie star like Debbie Reynolds."

The Nolans would invite my mother to the beverage room.

She always declined. My mother told me the Nolan sisters were as beautiful as Grace Kelly, but they both liked to take a drop or two and it would ruin their looks. She said they had an awful father who killed chickens and dogs. He left his daughters the house and at least they were able to make a living for themselves.

I adored the Nolan sisters who both wore pink and had a fondness for things gold that were available at Woolworth's. They knew how to keep a secret. A little boy from the neighbourhood and me watched each other pee in a flowerpot. I knew my mother would be furious but did not know why. One of the Nolans saw us but did not tell my mother.

That summer my grandmother died and at the wake my mother met Robert Smyth who was a widower. My mother was a young widow. She assured me she was not a spider.

The first time I met Robert I showed him a picture of my father and said, "That's my daddy."

My mother invited him for lunch and I was furious when she gave him half of my corn on the cob. In a rage, I did not eat.

Robert told us he was the only man in town who owned a television set. He said his new stereo played modern records. My mother's record player was old and played 78s.

Robert wanted to give my mother his daughter's set of the music to *Brigadoon*. His daughter was away in the city going to university. While we listened to the records, I wanted to be like the girl in the song whose hair hung down in ringlets. My mother sent Robert home with the records. They belonged to his daughter who was a smart girl and someday she would come home.

Robert invited us to go boating on the Ottawa River. My mother bought each of us a new bathing suit and packed a picnic lunch. The motorboat was docked at the marina and it took awhile for Robert to start the motor. Once we got on the river, he let me steer the boat for a short distance. Water surrounded our feet. Just as we were to go over the rapids, Robert stuck bubble gum in the hole and saved our lives. I told Robert and my mother a joke to ease the tension.

"What goes in hard and comes out soft?"

"Bubble gum."

Robert laughed.

I felt ashamed, even though I did not understand the meaning of the joke.

When I'd overheard the Nolan sisters tell my mother the joke, she'd laughed too.

Robert invited us to his house for Thanksgiving dinner. My mother made pounded potatoes, carrots with parsnips and roast beef for supper. My mother liked to "make things out of her head" and added radishes and green onions to the potatoes, and boiled the carrots in maple syrup.

There were some frozen blueberries that Robert had picked the summer before and he asked my mother to make a pie. She said she watched her mother have a stroke in her fifties because she made too many pies. She told Robert to make the pie himself or to buy one at the A&P.

I wanted to meet Robert's daughter, who was in a production of *Brigadoon* at university in Toronto. Robert said it cost him an arm and a leg to send her to school and she didn't have the decency to come home for Thanksgiving. The table was set with his deceased wife's pride and joy, her china and silver. She was a woman who knew how to bake a pie and how to handle her kids.

Dinner was served when Walt Disney started and I refused to come to the table.

My mother wanted to serve my Thanksgiving meal on a TV table but Robert said, "She has the run of you. Sit at the table. Now, Claire."

Robert turned off the TV set and we gave thanks at the table. I was forced to drink white milk rather than chocolate, which was what my mother served at our apartment.

That night I did not watch Ed Sullivan with my mother and

Robert. Instead I pretended to be sick and stayed in my bedroom.

When he drove us home to our apartment, which was at the other end of town, Robert said, "You don't belong to the jet set. When we get married, no more radishes in the potatoes. No wife of mine will be buying any pie at A&P."

I noticed Robert had hair growing out of his ears and nose.

At night my mother usually read to me before we said the Guardian Angel prayer and said goodnight. We slept in separate twin beds. My mother had a bad back and put a board on top of her mattress to help her pain. I did not get into bed with her when I had a nightmare.

That night she did not read a story. Instead she told me that when Robert went to confession, he always had a short penance, just three Hail Mary's at the most.

She said, "You learned an important lesson tonight, Claire. Men hate you and then they love you. That's just the way it is. Robert might be mean to us, but he will never hurt us."

When I went to confession, I made up my sins and always said I had disobeyed my mother three times. Sometimes after confession my mother had to say the rosary, which took a very long time.

My mother said, "Goodnight, my little angel."

They were married in a private mass in the palace, which was the house where the bishop lived. Neither myself nor Robert's daughter from his first marriage attended. My mother told me some people think widows who remarry are foolish and they had to have a quiet wedding. For their honeymoon my mother and Robert went to visit his daughter in Toronto. One of the Nolan sisters stayed with me at our apartment while they were away. She gave me some of her dresses and nighties to use for dress-up.

My bedroom in Robert's house was above the kitchen and off a summer sleeping room. There was a front and back stairway and my mother asked me to use the stairs closest to my room when I wanted a glass of milk at night. When I thought they were asleep,

I would go to the kitchen and come back upstairs with a glass of chocolate milk. I sat on the summer porch and told myself delicious, grand tales of my father's return. These imaginings fueled my nights alone in the back of the house.

On Wednesday evenings, my mother had her hair done and afterwards played bridge with some friends. I did not go with her to hair appointments. I stayed with Robert. I would put the music to *Brigadoon* on the record player, and play dress-up in the piano room. Robert usually watched television in the front of the house.

One night, Robert stood in the doorway of the piano room and said, "Claire, do you know what else goes in hard and come out soft?"

"Bubble gum," I said.

"Wrong."

The next day I walked to the Nolan sisters after school and asked if I could play with the curlers before I went home for supper. I told them I was afraid to go home. I told them that the night before I had gone to the kitchen down the back staircase and cooked the records from *Brigadoon*.

"Robert and my mother don't know yet and they'll be mad. I mean angry. Mom says only dogs can be mad."

"Claire, that's not what Debbie Reynolds would do. What possessed you to do such a thing?"

"My real daddy isn't coming back, is he?"

"No, honey."

When I got home, my mother had cleaned the oven.

She said, "The Nolans called. They told me what you said. Your real daddy is watching over you, angel. I won't tell Robert about the records. He won't notice. They were just 78s."

"Mom. What goes in hard and come out soft?" I asked.

"A frozen blueberry pie from A&P," she said.

A Prince is the Gift of Love

Fiona was certain her brother would have escaped the endless rapture of heaven to find adventure in the universe. She believed Matthew helped aliens negotiate their way around the planet. She and Matthew most often spoke late at night and sometimes he would fly by her bedroom window in a spaceship.

The familiar sound of a car pulling into the driveway signaled the return of her mother, from her early-bird swim at the Kiwanis Pool. After swimming twenty lengths of the pool, her mother would be "ready to start the day."

The year before, Matthew had taken the snowmobile out on the Ottawa River to check for fish at the hut. The snowmobile went through the ice and her younger brother went down with it. When he was alive, Fiona had not thought that much about Matthew, but since his death she had spent hours looking for him. Matthew would have been fifteen this year and Fiona had just turned sixteen.

A light rain was falling and it seemed a good day to stay home and do some sewing. If Matthew had lived, a drizzle would not have discouraged him.

One of the ways her mother contrived to get Fiona out of bed was to run a bath for her. While Fiona was in the tub, her mother made breakfast.

The daily knock at the bathroom door came and her mother said, "Fiona, you're going to be late for school."

"You're just afraid of me being alone in the nude, Mom."

Her mother had hated the snowmobile, an Arctic Cat, when Fiona's father bought it, but agreed because it could be another means of transportation to visit the cottage during the winter months. He would never be allowed to buy another.

The only time Fiona's mother had sat still since Matthew had died was when she was at mass. Her mother believed anything could be conquered with exercise, diet and communion.

Her mother had protested when Fiona took a part-time job at the Club Grill. She said it would interfere with her studies and sports. Her dad did not seem care about what she or her mom did since Matthew had died and Fiona missed her father, too, even though she saw him every day.

Fiona was able to make dresses by looking at pictures in *Seventeen* magazines and sometimes she would design her own clothes. Her mother did not approve of her sitting in front of the sewing machine when she could be doing sports.

Fiona's friends would ask her to make them dresses from pictures and she wondered if she might charge them. Her mother was not a seamstress and told her accepting money for sewing would be second class. Fiona asked her friends to buy her one lunch at the chip truck and to pay to go to the show once in exchange for a dress.

Matthew had been a good hockey player, but their mother was afraid his teeth would be knocked out. She encouraged him to focus on skiing, tennis and swimming.

Fiona's mother would send Fiona to the ski hill during an ice storm even if she had pneumonia. When her mother came into her bedroom, Fiona said, "There's a ski meet at Madawaska today, and I feel like staying home. The snow will be shitty."

While she gathered Fiona's clothes from the floor, Kate appeared perturbed.

"There are so many beautiful words in the English language. Please don't say shitty.

"Hurry up now. Your skis are ready to go at the back door."

After flossing and brushing her teeth twice, Fiona smiled a few times while looking in the bathroom mirror. She had worn braces and she was pleased with the results, even though the retainer had bothered her at night.

Wearing her baby-blue long underwear, Fiona sprayed Ambush perfume behind her ears and knees and braided her strawberry blonde hair. With her ski pants slung over her shoulder, Fiona went downstairs.

In the fridge she found the can of sugar-free juice. Her mother had banned sugar, white bread, and butter from the house since Matthew's death. There was a loaf wrapped in a tea towel in the refrigerator and Fiona dared not ask what it was, as she suspected it would be something ghastly.

"Can't you buy some decent juice? I miss Tang."

"You have nothing without your health, Fiona. Tang is loaded with sugar."

Her mother raised her hand to her forehead. Her cheeks were red and there were drops of perspiration on her face.

Fiona knew her mother would say the change of life was playing tricks on her because she had gone off her diet.

"You let your imagination run wild and it gets you in trouble. I thought I was having a heart attack for a second. Your grandmother always tempts me with her cooking."

Fiona poked at her overdone poached eggs.

"Life is sweet, Fiona, even though Matthew's not here."

Fiona's mind drifted. The week before, she had kissed Jimmy Cormier, a boy in her class who had a cold sore. She was worried that she might have VD. Because she would never be able to go to the doctor about it, she knew she would become disfigured and slowly sink into madness.

"Mom, I really don't want to race today. Charlie's Angels is on tonight and we'll be back late."

"Are you trying to kill me? You have to think of your team and the others. They come from far and wide for this race."

It was difficult to have a mother who might have a heart attack if her daughter did not go skiing on a rainy day.

"Which schools are competing, Fiona?"

While she stood in the centre of the kitchen, putting on her ski pants, Fiona said, "Lakefield College is one of the schools. Then just the regular schools."

"Fiona, I read in some magazine that Prince Andrew is at Lakefield this year. Isn't he a skier?"

"They'd drag a prince on a school bus to a hill that only has a T-bar? Guess Prince Andrew would think that was pretty neat. He's just from England."

Kate rinsed the breakfast dishes. "When you were a little, I asked you what a prince is and you said, 'A prince is the gift of love.' Funny, how you remember those things."

Fiona had hated the one day she worked at the Club Grill. The manager was a creep. He had told her that if she ever got pregnant she could talk to him.

After breakfast she asked her mother if she had seen her sketch pad and her mother replied, "You should be having fun with the other kids, Fiona. Not drawing on the bus."

Fiona had been fired from the Club Grill for refusing to wash the bathroom with Javex. She had accepted the job because she wanted to go to Ottawa to buy better fabric and *Italian Vogue*.

"Your dad brought a sandwich loaf home from his mother's. She made an extra one for her bridge club. I was going to throw it out but will pack some for your lunch today. But he thought he'd died and gone to heaven when she gave it to him."

"Everyone buys lunch at the hill."

"Five layers with ham, egg salad, cream cheese and cucumber fillings. It even has icing. Sinful. A thick sandwich cake."

"Can you pack some squares?"

"Sorry, no squares in this house."

"Mom, are you broke?"

"Just enough for your T-bar ticket, Sweetie. And that's a lot. There are kids who will never be able to ski."

Matthew died with his eyes wide open, in the deep black freezing Ottawa River, because of his father. That was what Fiona heard her mother say when she mentioned kids who could not ski. Her mother threw out the rest of Royal Sandwich Loaf.

"That's daddy's loaf!"

"Your daddy is my husband. We ate some last night and it's decadent."

Fiona did not know what decadent meant, but it sounded like a word that had more to do with sex than sandwiches.

The other members of the ski team looked as bleak as Fiona felt. Jimmy Cormier was on the bus. Fiona glanced at him and noticed that his cold sore had healed. When she walked by, he said, "Sit beside me, Dogface."

"How's your cold sore?"

He looked as if he might cry.

Fiona then ignored him and looked for her friend Lisa, but Lisa wasn't on the bus. Fiona sat at the back and took out her sketchbook.

Fiona often thought of other ways her brother might have died and wanted to stop all dangers that still lurked for him and for her. She sometimes saw what others did not, and that surprised boys who thought she would be more like how they imagined a girl who could be on a milk commercial.

At sixteen, Fiona refused to take a typewriting class so that she could never become a secretary and she did not want to find herself going up the aisle with Jimmy Cormier someday. She had kissed him back and it was fun, but he was still just Jimmy Cormier to her. Like heaven, he was boring.

Sometimes, when her mother cut her dad with her words, she would say a sweet lie to soften the wound.

Fiona didn't understand why Jimmy had called her Dogface, but she was not going to be sweet to him again.

The schedule for the slalom races was posted inside the dining hall. Saint Columba was racing first and Lakefield College was to compete in the afternoon.

Fiona bought a pack of Thrills gum and applied Bain de Soleil for luck. Thrills gum and Bain de Soleil were as much a part of skiing as her expensive equipment, equipment charged by her mother, who had been hiding the bills from her father.

The snow was packed and Fiona wished the races had been held at Mount Saint Marie or at least a hill that had a chair lift. The team said a Hail Mary prior to the race. As Jimmy Cormier wiped out at the third gate, Fiona saw a green and white coach pull into the parking lot, which was filled with yellow school buses.

When her turn came, Fiona managed not to knock over any poles and to keep the tips of both skies between the gates. While she made her way slowly down the hill, without any concern for winning, she thought of her brother Matthew who would be shouting at her, Fiona, move your butt. She asked Matthew to arrange for her to ski with Andrew if he was at the race.

The Royal Sandwich slice had not survived the trip in one piece, but Fiona was hungry and had no choice but to eat the mushy mess. She ate the cream cheese icing with her fingers.

Fiona doubted her vision when she thought she saw Prince Andrew sitting at one of the picnic tables inside the chalet beside an older, fit man and some other Lakefield College students. The alleged prince was eating chips and gravy.

The girls who were at the ski meet were eager to meet private school boys, but it seemed Fiona was the only one who guessed a prince was there. She had for years enjoyed looking at photos of the Royal Family in *Life* magazine, especially when she was in the bathroom.

Fiona wondered if the prince was given his privacy because, even though he was recognizable, it seemed impossible for him to be at this ski hill on racing day.

The building they called the chalet was used as a bar at night. For the races, the owner had arranged for embarrassing entertainment. The McCool Band was playing their original song,

"Johnny's Pickup." As the prince and his security guard walked towards the washroom, Andrew looked over at the band, which was now playing "The Potato Serenade." Fiona resisted the urge to follow Andrew into the men's washroom, but waited in the boot change room.

A few minutes later, Fiona positioned herself a few people away from where Prince Andrew sat on the bench. She undid her braids and let her wavy red hair free. Her mother had often told her that her ears were not her best feature.

Fiona leaned over to do up her boots at the same time as Andrew did his. His head was lowered and, with her well-practiced smile, Fiona tried to capture the eye of someone from the House of Windsor.

Fiona declined the T-bar, left the line, and waited for Prince Andrew to move into place to go up the hill.

The overweight guy who was directing traffic at the T-bar did not offer Prince Andrew first place in the lineup. Fiona managed to get behind the Prince and his security guard.

When the prince and his guard reached the front of the line, and the attendant held out the T-bar for them, Fiona moved quickly into the security guard's place. Prince Andrew was startled but turned to the guard as the they moved forward with Fiona at his side, and said, "Go for tea. I'll be fine."

The prince smiled and introduced himself as Andrew and Fiona felt a goof when she said, "You can call me Fiona."

Mesmerized by his speaking voice, Fiona felt as though she were dreaming when she watched Andrew's skis moving in the grooves on the track and wondered if he thought she was beautiful.

"Isn't this the most beautiful hill in the world, Andrew?"

Prince Andrew laughed and Fiona noticed that his teeth were not as perfect as hers. "I've skied in Austria and all over the world. But, yes. This is a nice hill."

"You have to be careful on Coulas Chute," she said. "It's

dangerous because the owners haven't gotten around to digging up all the rocks, and it has a patch that's always icy."

Fiona dared to look directly into his brown eyes because she wanted him to notice her blue eyes that she had been told were beautiful. Fiona's hair was blowing in her face and her ears were hidden.

She noticed his red toque that was the kind of thing her mother would put her nose up at. While she considered his headwear, Fiona inquired how Andrew enjoyed Canada. Then she asked, "Do they play tennis in England?"

The prince smiled and said, "Wimbledon."

"Oh my God. I forgot about Wimbledon and I'm a tennis player."

"Are you going to play at the Toronto Open?" he asked.

With an infectious laugh, Fiona showed off her sparkling teeth.

"No," she said. She marveled that Andrew thought she might be such a good player.

It saddened her that, even with a prince, she was afraid he might ask about her family, but wanted to ask after his.

Fiona looked at his hat and could not bear it any longer.

"I like your toque. Did someone knit it?"

"Yes. My grandmother did, before I came to Canada."

"Holy cow, the Queen Mother, that's so neat," said Fiona.

She melted when the prince said, "Grandmothers are a gift."

Fiona hesitated because it might seem that she was lying if she told the prince her grandmother had made a Royal Sandwich Loaf. Instead she said, "My grandmother made the sandwich I packed for lunch. She's as smart as a whip."

She was wearing Matthew's ski mitts. Fiona touched the lining of the mitt hoping to bring her brother's attention to her time with a prince who was wearing a red toque, and who was listening to her talk about their beloved grandmother. She and Andrew had something in common.

When they had reached the top of the hill Fiona did not want to let go of the T-bar. "Do you want to race?"

Prince Andrew said, "Thank you, but my team is meeting at the Chute. If time permitted, I would most assuredly race with you, and no doubt, you would win."

A scowling security guard got off the next T-bar. Andrew smiled at Fiona and said, "Oh. He followed me. Cheerio, Fiona."

With the strap of her pole wrapped around her wrist, Fiona threw kisses at Prince Andrew's back while he skied towards Coulas Chute and said, "A prince is the gift of love."

Mock Duck

The change had come late to Eva Owens. The women who belonged to her Wednesday afternoon book club were suspicious of her because the curse visited her like clockwork until she was fifty-three-years old. For a while it had been a dribble, some months nothing, and then it finally was over.

Two of the women in the club were replacements for members who had gone to an early grave. One had died of breast cancer five years before and another, as everyone knew but did not say, died from her own hand by taking a bottle of Valium. She was a woman who had everything to live for and Eva had not forgiven her for what she had put her family through.

The newest member of the book club, Alice Breen, worked as a theatre director in Toronto. She was visiting Saint Columba for a few months to care for her mother. Alice was thought to have a girlfriend in the city, and when she and Eva were in grade school they had shared a couple of kisses, playing mommy and daddy. Eva could not recall who she had played. She wondered if Alice remembered their game.

Alice knew Eva's most cherished secret; she could not trust that Alice would not let slip something about her long-ago affair with Tommy Daley.

Eva knew she should feel remorse over her time with Tommy Daley, but she did not. When Eva was at home alone with two young kids while her husband was away for six months at a time, training horses across the country and in the U.S., Tommy would drop by with his guitar and serenade Eva. He had reminded her of Marlon Brando, wearing his white t-shirts and Levi's jeans.

Alice had witnessed Eva and Tommy in a compromising position one summer evening —in, of all places, the cemetery — and even though it had been two decades since that evening, Alice had happened upon them when Eva was climaxing and she knew Alice was there because she had roared with laughter before she ran off into the night.

For their twenty-fifth wedding anniversary, Eva and her husband had received a plaque from the diocese commemorating their quarter century of marriage. A party was held for them at the church hall. Racing and boxing were the only things that compelled Eva's husband to travel with her and, to celebrate, he took her to New York to go to the track.

They were at Belmont on July 6, 1975 when that the great filly Ruffian broke down in a match race against the colt Foolish Pleasure. Eva remembered watching in horror as the filly faltered after the first half-mile, and she cried when they had to put her down the next day after a failed attempt to repair the ankle. Everyone, except perhaps Lou, was traumatized by the elegant Ruffian's screeches. That horse was something special.

The race at Belmont was Eva's introduction to feminism. She and Lou wore buttons. Hers was for Ruffian and Lou, of course, was wearing his button for Foolish Pleasure. Gloria Steinem was at the race along with other trailblazers who were there for Ruffian. Eva read about Gloria and Betty Friedan in the New York papers and, when she returned to Canada, she bought a copy of The Feminine Mystique.

For Eva, menopause was the end of her girlhood and she feared she would not make a good old wise woman. She feared she had not yet begun to live her life and soon it could end. She feared it was too late for everything. She was grateful that Tommy had given her passion. At least she knew sex was more than staring at the ceiling waiting for your man to have his way with you. But Lou had satisfied her financial needs, which were more important than passion, she thought.

Since Lou's death, Eva had been particularly nervous at night.

She changed the sheets once during the night because of sweating. She was reading *The Exorcist* for her book club that was meeting in two days, and she left her bed to sleep on the couch.

The novel terrified her and she turned on all of the lights in the house and cowered all night on the couch. In the morning, while she was drinking her coffee, she listed the places her husband had hidden his extra money. She knew she had not found it all.

In many ways Eva Owens lived for the dead, and today, Easter Sunday was the first anniversary of her husband's untimely tragic death at the age of fifty-two. He had been a healthy man, but smoked two packs of Peter Jacksons a day. Eva didn't miss the smell of smoke in the house. Even though she herself had never taken a puff, all of her clothes and bedding still carried the scent of smoke. She liked to say he was a magnificent man, which to her ears suggested her husband had been virile, strong and smart. Lou could now be whoever Eva wanted him to be.

To acknowledge his death, Eva went to morning mass on Easter, made a visit to the cemetery, and planned to make his favorite dish, mock duck, for dinner.

Their eldest son, Joseph, was working in Labrador in a mine after quitting Mount Allison where he had gone on a football scholarship. A daughter, Mona, was travelling in Greece, and her youngest, Violet, born a "mongoloid," was living at Rideau Regional Hospital in Smiths Falls. Violet was well taken care of and since she had been three years old, Eva had visited her baby girl faithfully every second Sunday, and at Christmas, Easter and Thanksgiving for the last fifteen years. But this year she had not seen Violet since the summer months. Eva had not told her that the man she called "Daddy" had joined the silent majority.

The shame of Violet was not her Down syndrome, but the

question of her paternity. Eva, Lou and Tommy Daley had always known who Violet's father was. Nonetheless, Violet Bernadette Owens was baptized and on the birth certificate Lou Owens was listed as the father.

For many years, Lou had little tolerance for Violet's presence. She was an unusually sweet but stubborn child.

The doctor who had delivered Violet waited three years before he told Eva she was what he called "a mongoloid child." Everyone except Eva knew the moment they laid eyes on Violet that she had Down Syndrome. The adulterous Eva saw a beautiful blue-eyed toddler who needed to catch up, but she found it hard to believe anything was wrong with Violet. The doctor told her there was nothing in Saint Columba for Violet. He told her Violet would be too hard on the other children.

Like Violet, Eva was stubborn and would never have agreed to send her away, but she needed to keep her husband at home to pay the bills.

Joseph, who was then four years old, let the cat out of the bag when he said to his father, "Tommy sleeps in Mom's bed to scare away the bears."

Lou threatened to kill Tommy with a knife but, in the end, Tommy Daley, out of respect for Eva's marriage, left town, only to return fourteen years later to be buried. Violet was born six months after Tommy's sudden departure.

Lou Owens died on Easter Sunday in 1976. That morning, Eva woke to find her husband lying on the floor. His face was blue, but he was alive. Lou was fifty-two years old. He whispered, "Call the doctor," and she said, "I can't. The doctor is dead."

It was maybe the dumbest thing she had ever said, but it was true that the only doctor, the man who had delivered every baby in town since the war, had died of a stroke on Valentine's Day of that year.

While Eva stood and watched her husband die, she thought about Tommy Daley dying on an icy road – a beautiful man, the father of her lovely Violet, driving a logging truck in northern British Columbia – dead within minutes. She did not lean over to touch her husband, nor did she call anyone for help. She stood in her bare feet, noticing that her toenails needed to be trimmed. She was wearing a pink nightgown Lou had bought her at the five-and-dime for her birthday.

Lou was gone shortly after she had finished telling him the doctor was dead, but she just stood there, frozen, her feet going numb on the hardwood floor. The day before, the cleaning woman, whom her husband had loathed, had waxed the floors, and the clean smell of lemon remained. How fortuitous it was that Eva had also asked her to clean the silver, because she knew they would come from far and wide to attend his funeral and the house was ready for the onslaught of mourners.

The fear of acknowledging the truth was perhaps driven by a perverse politeness. Eva heartily agreed with this means of maintaining order and civility. She longed to visit Tommy's grave, but did not want to draw attention, and sometimes she would stroll by his tombstone. He was buried next to his great aunt whom he had barely known. This day she had a potted African violet to leave for Tommy.

It seemed like it took hours for her husband to die and that was what she told everyone at his funeral, but really he had lain there helpless wearing his striped pajamas for only about five minutes. Eva could not know if his life flashed before his eyes, but while he lay on the freshly waxed hardwood floor she thought of the horses he had killed over the years to boost their livelihood.

She had benefited a lot from his secret profession, but they had always been careful because most people would have wondered how they did so well. He could make a standard bred trot like no one else. And he travelled across the country and into the States to give a little help to owners who could not afford to keep a horse that wasn't a winner.

Her husband knew the best methods to put down the best of them, jumpers who belonged to blue bloods who lived in King City, cutting horses that performed at the Calgary Stampede. Any poor horse that was valuable enough to destroy.

Even though Lou would have died if she had called an ambulance when she found him, she secretly believed that she had killed her husband. She had imagined this moment with hope for the future: Lou dead of a heart attack. Who would blame her for living on after him? Some would applaud her courage and dignity when she did not break down and cry like a foolish girl.

Eva appreciated the extra money, which he told her had hidden throughout the house. He would get a cut of the insurance payout and sometimes that was a handsome sum. Other times not so much. A few times he was contracted to kill horses for spite. A man who lived in upstate New York wanted his wife's horses of no record gone, just because she loved them.

The last meal Lou had eaten was mock duck with mashed potatoes and creamed corn. It was his favourite. He had belonged to the Knights of Columbus, coached the hockey team, collected the offerings at mass on Sunday mornings; he would visit invalids and help anyone who asked him. He was a dutiful man and regularly made the drive to Smiths Falls to visit Violet. Even though he could never really accept her, as she got older, he looked forward to seeing Violet, who was quite charming. They did bring their other kids with them to see her but told them not to talk about her at school or to their friends.

After she visited her men at the cemetery, she would make mock duck, mashed potatoes and creamed corn for dinner – like a man, one who knew his way around horses, and always ate dinner alone.

Alice Breen walked past the cemetery entrance wearing a track suit and running shoes. She was out of breath. She looked much younger than her fifty-some years and Eva was embarrassed by the way she herself had aged. Alice had had an easy life, Eva decided. Who wouldn't if they did not have a heavy-handed man about the place?

During the last year, Eva had gained fifty pounds. Every round steak filled with dressing wrapped in bacon added to her wide girth. It was frightening to Eva. She was five seven and had always been thin and now she was afraid to have jar of peanut butter in the house because she would stand in front of the refrigerator at two a.m. and eat half a jar with a spoon.

Eva felt conspicuous in the new size eighteen cloth coat she had bought at the Hudson Bay store in Montreal two weeks before. Lou had told her she should not show off their money too much. A trainer would not make enough to buy such a fancy coat.

She did not miss Lou, but felt it would be noticed if she didn't do what a grieving widow should do.

Eva said to Alice, "Come and visit Lou with me." The ground was wet and muddy, but the sun was shining and it was a beautiful April day.

"When is the next book club meeting?" Alice asked. "I heard you want me banned. It's not until September. I took leave to refresh myself. The club is fun. What's next on the list, *The Glorification of Al Toonie*? Who's even heard of it? Go easy on me, Eva. You are not a saint and Lou? Well, he was as cold as the ice on the river in January, but he stayed with you. But you already know that."

Eva held her unbuttoned coat together and said without tears, "Terrible, terrible thing to say on the anniversary of my husband's death. Why in God's name would you say such a thing?"

Eva felt strangely comfortable with this woman whom she had known for years and who knew some of her secrets.

Alice laughed and said, "You know I know, Eva."

"No clue what you are talking about. Alice, you've lived in the city for so long. Did you know – or at least, I have heard – that if a woman knows a man has a handgun and he shoots someone with it she can go to prison along with him, even though she didn't pull the trigger?"

"That's ridiculous, but I believe it happens. But how is Violet? These days you know they're closing places like the institution she lives in and bringing them home or to the cities to live in the free world."

One of Eva's shoes dug into the mud and she was not on an even keel. She realized it was pointless to try to impress Alice Breen with how well she bore the burden of her husband's death.

No one had asked after Violet in years. Eva wanted to cry. "She doesn't know Lou is dead yet. He grew to love her, you know. She's quite the bowler, and she takes after me: she likes clothes. But with Violet everything has to be pink."

Alice asked, "Did Tommy Daley ever meet Violet?"

Eva took both of her high heels off and said, "No. Lou would have killed him and me. Tommy never married, you know."

"Not the type to settle down. Tommy had a magnificent voice. It's tragic he wasn't able to bring his talent to the world."

"Would you like to come to dinner? I'm making mock duck. I have photos of Violet you can look at. She is a beautiful girl."

Hope

Dear Darcy,

On the surface of things, it seems as though I fucked Phil over. He did give me a leg up by paying for my flight to Athens. But he doesn't really want me to be a playwright. He just wants me to get the idea out of my system. Go to Greece, realize you can't cut it, and come back and spend the rest of your life in Toronto.

    I guess he blabbed to everyone that I broke his nose the night before I left. It just sort of happened. Phil's a wacko, wanting to marry a drunk like me. But thanks to that detour with him, I've found peace of mind. When I got kicked off the bus, I just stayed in Toronto instead of going to Vancouver. If Phil had not introduced himself at People's Restaurant, I would have gone west. He trapped me with his welcoming ways and it took a year to break away.

    During the last three months, Sophocles, Thucydides and Euripides have saved my life. I know this without having even read their poems. I'm now on a truly glorious path and severed from all those fucking cowshit valley values.

    Have I mentioned Saul? He lives in a renovated goat house and prefers the company of gypsies. He hasn't gone home to New York for over thirty years. Saul's a poet. A proudly unpublished poet.

    He and I make fun of the North Americans with their knapsacks and guitars. They travel just to hang out with each other and to compete for passport stamps from different countries.

    I just got back from Istanbul. I went there to have my visa renewed for another three months. The Greek authorities told me to leave the country because I am financially embarrassed. It was Saul's idea and it worked. They re-stamped my passport when I came back and now I can legally stay here for three more months.

At the Topaki Place, I met a man who carried a stick and at the border one of the guards had a pet rooster. None of that tourist shit for me.

It isn't a sexual thing between Saul and me. He mostly sits on a bench in the National Park drinking brandy. And sometimes I join him. He understands that I'm a writer even though I haven't put down a word of dialogue since I got off the plane. Like Saul, I don't want to go back to a middle-of-the-road world filled with disapproving looks. Sorry. I guess that's your world.

For the first time in years I'm more or less sober. They serve olives and feta cheese with a shot of ouzo and it's a good way to have a cheap lunch. Whatever happens to me here, I know about it before anyone else tells me.

I saw a French film about a guy who cuts off his dick so that he and the woman he loves would be equals. That's the kind of guy I want to meet. The kind of guy who would cut off his dick to make his woman feel more comfortable. A real blow up guy.

A Greek film, Medea, is superb. Best to see it without English subtitles.

Wealthy bankers dominate the world and everyone is a con. How do we know we are really here, anyway?

Booze is cheap here. I've a reputation in the bars in the Plaka. They suspect I belong to the CIA.

I have peace of mind.

Love, Mona

After she paid for her breakfast, a double Greek coffee, two beers and a spanakopita, Mona, who didn't know a Darcy, folded the thin blue paper, put it in an airmail envelope and scribbled, "Darcy Magee, Saint John's Newfoundland." Mona's address book was filled with made-up names and addresses. Now she would go across the street from Syntagma Square to American Express to pick up her mail and send her correspondence to Canada.

A few weeks before, on her twenty-fourth birthday, Mona had written to Phil, whose name and address she had not made up, and asked his forgiveness for breaking his nose and to front her five hundred dollars until she got on her feet as a writer. It was strange he had not responded, and Mona wondered if he might be dead. She needed a cheque from Phil. There were ten twenty-dollar traveller's cheques left to live on for the next three months. While she waited in the lineup, Mona convinced herself that Phil had sent a grand instead. She thought about taking another trip to Istanbul with the money. She would leave that afternoon and not go back to the pension at Omonia Square.

There was a letter from Canada, but it wasn't from Phil. A school tour from the convent she had attended as a girl in the Ottawa Valley was coming to Athens and Sister Celestine wanted to arrange to meet. Mona's mother had insisted the nun contact her. This was a dreadful invitation, but Mona remembered the nun fondly, perhaps because she was a woman who had been deprived of her dreams.

Sister Celestine had entered the convent because she wanted to be a missionary. The order would not send her to South America because she had her own ways and might cause trouble. The sisters were embarrassed when Sister Celestine took it upon herself to visit men in the local jail and then meet them for pizza at the Rawhide Restaurant on Main Street when they were released. Mona found it curious that the Grey Sisters had sent a group of students to Greece with Sister Celestine.

The nun had been her Grade 10 Latin teacher. Mona could no longer conjugate a Latin verb, but she would never forget the story of Matthew Talbot. Even though he had died in 1925 while walking on a Dublin street after mass, Matt Talbot was a man after Sister Celestine's heart. She had been relentless in her campaign to have Matthew Talbot made a saint. The little man who had lived in Dublin, Ireland was a dipsomaniac who had gotten himself off the piss with God's help in 1884.

Matt Talbot was twelve when he started to drink and, after a horrendous sixteen years, he got sober with the help of a priest. After that he got work in the timber yards and was "very strong in the rights of the working man."

Mona had been fifteen when she'd had her first drink, a bottle of homemade dandelion wine, eleven years before.

She thought of Sister Celestine. Four years earlier, Mona had sent the nun a letter of congratulations, after reading in a newspaper that Matt Talbot had been made venerable. He wasn't a saint yet, but was on his way to canonization. Now that it had been acknowledged, in 1973, that this Irish drunk was a model of holiness, and had been given the title of "venerable," it would have to be proven that a miracle occurred after his death as a result of someone praying to him for Matthew Talbot to be beatified. The final step, in order to be canonized a saint, was to prove that a second miracle had occurred

Mona walked to Kolonaki, where she thought she was more likely to meet someone who would buy her a drink. It was an upscale neighbourhood of the city where there were few backpackers.

Sister Celestine would arrive in Athens in three days. She thought of the nun lecturing her for tardiness in the tenth grade.

"Consistency, Mona. Matt Talbot said that what God wants from us are consistency and constancy."

Mona understood that in her life neither could exist, and that she could easily not make it to lunch with the nun.

A hustler she recognized from the bars was sitting at a table in the square drinking coffee. She was surprised to see him in this section of Athens and went over to his table.

"Aren't you Billy? Saul knows you."

"The American drunk."

"He's an expatriate poet," said Mona.

Mona knew that Billy would most likely ask her to buy him lunch because he forgot his wallet at home. She wanted him to buy her a drink.

Billy ran his fingers through his hair, took his keys from his pocket and twirled the key chain as though he were thinking of another woman.

"I'm having a bad day, Billy. I'm going to have to find a job."

"You are most welcome to join my table. Has anyone spoken to you of your friend, Saul?"

"Everything sounds so fucking important when you don't use contractions," she said.

"Saul is dead. I am sorry."

Mona opened her purse and touched the letter she had received from Sister Celestine. She was amazed when she noticed that her purse was laden with change and signaled for the waiter.

"How would you know?"

"A butcher in the market told me this morning. Saul owed us money," Billy said.

"Can you give me a minute, here? Was he alone?"

"Of course. He died in his goat house. His stomach was sick and he did not wake up."

Mona glanced at Billy's short haircut and polished shoes. He was a man who took pride in his appearance. Saul was an old man. Older than he really was. There were three stray sugar cubes on the table and Mona wondered how they had fallen from Billy's saucer. She thought of Saul. Like Mona, he could not pretend to be part of polite society. When he was drunk, he did not know what would happen. Mona wondered if Saul knew he was dead.

Mona wished she had woken to the smell of homemade beans baking in a slow oven. Baked beans were the food of Good Friday and funerals.

"What will happen to Saul? I mean where will he be buried?"

Billy shrugged his shoulders.

"Saul had a secret. He told everyone he grew up on the Lower East Side. But he was from New Jersey. His father made a lot of money building shopping malls. They sent him money every month and I guess they'll bring him home," she said.

"I can offer you employment. But we must fuck," Billy said.

The waiter finally came to their table. He was dressed in a white shirt and black pants and seemed to Mona to represent all the waiters who mistake their patrons to be a reflection of who they are. He overheard Billy's request and Mona felt that this middle-aged man may as well be a nun from the Ottawa Valley.

"Do you have any brandy at your place, Billy?"

"I don't drink. Have one here. Where is your home, in Canada?"

"Nowhere. I move around a lot. The last place I lived was Toronto. I told you Saul's secret. Now, I'll tell you mine. I say I am a writer. But it's more of a case of appearances. I like to say I'm a writer. But I only write bullshit letters to strangers."

"My uncle lives in Toronto. He owns a fur shop, Canada Furs. I would like to visit there someday," he said.

"Let's get out of here. It's time to go. We can pick up a bottle."

Billy's room smelled of pee and the men's cologne Old Leather. Mona was alarmed when Billy told her his age. After she drank a bottle of brandy it no longer mattered that he was five years younger than her.

When she woke up in Billy's room the next morning there was another man in bed with her. Billy was pacing around the room fully clothed and the other man was sleeping.

Mona sat on the edge of the mattress. She noticed menstrual blood on her thighs and on the mattress. Billy stood in front of her, took a knife out of his pocket, and held it to her throat.

"I'm Billy, and I'm sadistic and masochistic. The brandy is gone."

"May as well just slit my throat then," she said.

Death was often followed by gifts of food to the mourning family and her mother would always make beans, scalloped potatoes, and coleslaw for those who had lost loved ones.

Billy laughed and asked her to meet him that night at the

American Restaurant. It was the place where they served hamburgers and played The Mamas and the Papas on the sound system. Billy wanted Mona to turn tricks for him. For a couple of nights' work she could make enough money for a return ticket to Istanbul. He told her that in ancient Greece prostitution was legal, but it no longer was. Billy told her to take a shower before she came to work.

Mona was alarmed. She was not in the habit of sleeping with younger men.

"Saul says guys like you, who work the tourists, don't have a choice. Thanks for the offer, Billy, but I'm not like you. There's no way I could hold down a job."

Like Matthew Talbot, Sister Celestine supported unions and had encouraged her students to protest and to practice self-sacrifice for a larger cause. Mona could not imagine being strong on the rights of anyone.

"Meet me tonight at the American Restaurant."

Mona remembered that Matt Talbot had frequented ladies of the night before he got sober. She had derived her knowledge of Matthew Talbot from writing letters to the Vatican on Sister Celestine's behalf. It was a requirement for all Grade 10 Latin students. They would each take turns staying after school to compose pleas to make venerable the Irish man who got sober with God's help. Mona wrote the most enthusiastic letters and it was her responsibility to walk to the post with the package at the end of each week. The clandestine operation came to an end when the parish priest demanded that all communication on the matter cease.

A few days later Mona woke in a room she was not familiar with. She was terrified and tried to remember what day it was. This kind of shit was only supposed to happen in Canada. She looked around the room and saw signs that someone, a guy, lived there. There were some shirts thrown on a chair, shaving cream on the sink and cowboy boots near the door.

She saw a pot of white beans soaking on the night table. She knew this was imagined, but it seemed so real, she could see floating bits of bean jackets in the water. She wished the beans were baking in an oven absorbing the mixture of maple syrup, dry mustard, a little chopped onion and salt pork. For Saul, she would have replaced the pork with lamb.

Music was coming from the radiator and Mona strained to hear. She recognized what she thought was a Bee Gees tune. Mona was shaking too much to pick up a glass of water. She couldn't recall if the Bee Gees, a band she loathed, had done "Can't Live." She craved baked beans and a bottle of brandy. The room was moving.

A paperback with a pink elephant on the cover was on the bed beside her. The men she met in Athens were not big drinkers and she wondered why one of them would buy an English book on alcoholism. She imagined whoever he was was out buying them croissants and coffee for breakfast. She had a fragment of a memory of a guy wearing flannel pajamas sleeping beside her the night before. If he did not return before she left, Mona knew she would never know who he was.

There was a typewriter floating around the room and a piece of paper flew out of it. Mona believed it was her soul leaving her. She was twenty-six and knew without reading the Penguin book on alcoholism that she was seeing things that were not there. A portion of a quote from Matt Talbot, "When alone guard your thoughts," circled in her mind and she laughed at the impossibility of such a notion. She wondered if Matt Talbot's mother made homemade beans on Fridays, as her mother had done.

She smelled like a draft room on Sunday morning. The crotch of her jeans was caked in menstrual blood. Mona tried to remember how many days she had been away from her room in Omonia Square. Her period had stopped and it must have been at least five days. In the bathroom sink she soaked her Levi's for a few minutes before putting them on.

The brightness of the morning was unbearable. She walked by some Canadians and the feeling that she was worthy of their judgment was heavy. She had missed lunch with Sister Celestine and the students from Our Lady's. Although Mona's purse was heavy with change, she did not have any traveller's cheques left to pay rent.

When he died, forty years after his last drink, Matt Talbot's friends and family were surprised to learn that he had chains fastened around his waist, knee and right arm as a reminder to be true to God, Our Lord Jesus, and the Blessed Mother. Sister Celestine provided her students with copies of articles written in the *Irish Times* in 1925. The newspaper picked up on the story of a sinner who found redemption using pain and the ways of the Franciscans.

Even though no one knew Mona at the pension in the Plaka, she was afraid to go back there. There were empty bottles of brandy and retsina stacked in the closet of her room. She was afraid the cleaning staff had discovered them.

She needed to sit beside Saul on his bench in the park, but he wasn't at the National Park. Maybe his body really had been shipped home to New Jersey. She sat on the bench and hummed the theme song to the *Unsinkable Molly Brown*, and then drank water from a fountain and wondered what happened to drunks in Ancient Greece. Mona decided that most likely they went to Delphi or else they died. She knew that Saul had died.

When Saul first came to Athens, he had tried to escape the prevalence of drink in his life. Then he realized he could not take his place in society because he was a warrior. His spirit needed to drink because it was where he belonged. Booze was his home. People like him and Mona were spat on, but they were really prophets who told the truth. He and Mona agreed that maybe life was a dream and that there was no way to really prove that we are really here on earth.

She realized she had no one left to be alone with. She was an alcoholic and there was no use in trying any more to take her place in the world. There was a feeling of freedom in deciding to just be who she was born to be and inherit Saul's place on the bench. She wondered how she could sit there for another twenty years. She wondered again if you could die and not know it.

Mona desperately wanted to meet up with her Grade 10 Latin teacher. She wanted to be fifteen again and not lose her head to any drink that came her way. She wanted to walk into her home and smell baked beans. There was a good chance that Mona's smell and demeanour would not disgust Sister Celestine.

From Saul's bench, she could see the National Library, and Mona thought of all the books she had not read. She thought of herself when she was fifteen, when she wrote letters to Rome begging for Matthew Talbot to be beatified. Matt had said that it was easier to get out of hell than it was to stop drinking.

Mona said out loud, "I want to start walking and never stop. I want to walk the edge of the earth. Who the fuck am I kidding? Saul's dead and I am fucked. I'll spend the next thirty years alone and drunk on this bench. My family couldn't afford to ship my body home."

At the hotel where Sister Celestine was staying, Mona learned that she and the students had checked out.

"Will she be back? I have to see her. I can't go back to Canada and I can't stay here."

The woman behind the desk shook her head and said, "No. They are leaving from Jerusalem for Canada."

She asked the madame if Sister Celestine had mentioned having a dream that one of her former charges was at the butcher's market, where she had been hung beside the slaughtered goats and lambs.

Madame Cleo had liked Sister Celestine and told Mona she would rent her a room, on credit, for the night, because it would make the sister happy. The space Sister Celestine had stayed in was available. This suited Mona. She tried to smell the nun's defiance when she walked in the door. It was a tiny room with a balcony that looked out on the busy Plaka.

Mona ran a bath in a gas-heated tub. She wanted to cry but could not. She stood on the tile while the tub filled. She prayed that an apparition would appear. A woman dressed in a white lace dress or a gentle man. Then she hoped that Saul would walk through the door. Mona was alone in the bathroom.

She wondered if Saul could see her now that he was dead. She wondered if he knew that, like her, he had left life long before he stopped drinking. He had been long dead, but Matthew Talbot still needed something to earn him sainthood.

Under her left breast, Mona noticed an open sore that was the size of a penny. It was screaming with infection. It must have caused pain but Mona did not feel any. There was a feeling of déjà vu when for the second time that week Mona saw a typewriter on the wall. A sheet of paper rolled itself loose and faded into the steamy air. Even though Mona knew what she had just witnessed was as a result of delirium tremens, she also believed that the delusion was the venerable Irish man's way of saying hi.

"Matthew Talbot, help me. If you can stop my drinking, I can be that miracle you need. You give me something and I'll give you what you need."

She put her hand on her throat and thought of Billy and his knife. It seemed to her that Billy was an okay guy and that he was only joking.

"Bring hope to my heart. I cannot go on like this and I cannot stop drinking. You and I know that I'm an alcoholic. Moving to another city, like Istanbul, is not going to work. There are no more leaves to turn over. You said it's easier to get out of hell than to quit drinking. I'm tired. Canada is a write-off, because I don't want anyone to see me like this. I don't want anyone to remember what I did the last time they saw me. Your heavy-handed words, 'Three things I cannot escape, the eye of God, the voice of conscience, and the stroke of death,' frighten me. But if you help me to get sober, I'll campaign my ass off to have you beatified."

She fell asleep in the warm water. When she woke, Mona felt there was a chain around her waist, her knee and her right arm. She touched the iron and wept.

Even if she could not prove it to the Vatican, Mona knew that Matthew Talbot, the man after her own heart, had his miracle. She was amazed.

During her remaining three months in Athens, Mona managed to hold down a job. Billy paid Mona handsomely for her reliable, sober work.

Every day, Mona wrote to Rome, demanding the beatification of Matthew Talbot.

Irish Soda Bread

Verna Dingle knew the difference between Ireland and the Ottawa Valley. The Saint Patrick's Day parade, afternoon tea, and the stage play in the evening were annual traditions attended by everyone in town.

Verna Dingle was most sought after by both the organizers of the tea and Saint Columba's Little Theatre Group. She was from Dublin, where she had met her husband during the war. Verna Dingle had once appeared in a play at the Abbey Theatre. Everyone in Saint Columba knew this story through Verna's husband, Aloysius, who was very proud of his striking wife. However cruel he was to her in private, she was his proof of her husband's worldliness and wonder.

The only keepsakes Verna brought with her from Ireland were playbills from the National Theatre. The ads in the playbills for places like Jacob's Patricia Chocolates, Kennedy's bread, ads written in Irish, reminded her of home and her mother who was still alive but aging in Dublin.

Verna had studied at Trinity College in Dublin, where she obtained a degree in Archeology. When she came to Canada she thought her degree would be useless until she developed an interest in the Algonquin Indians who had once inhabited the land where she now lived. Since she had moved from Dublin to Saint Columba she had collected artifacts and had fought for the protection of a native burial ground.

Every year Verna made Irish soda bread to be served with

lamb stew after the Saint Patrick's Day play. The tea was also a demand on her time. It was considered an honour to sit at the head of the table and pour the tea from the silver teapot.

Her eldest child, Grace, had been part of the entertainment at the tea the previous year. When she step-danced, Grace moved her arms in the way of Ottawa valley dancers, and Verna winced. She had taught her five children to dance the Irish way with their arms held straight.

After the concert, she said to Grace, "You looked like an elephant up there."

Verna tapped Grace on the head and said, "Go away with you – you know your mother loves you."

There was a rumour in town that Verna often beat her children to a pulp whether they needed it or not.

This year Verna planned to beg off the Saint Patrick's Day tea and would send her sister-in-law, Sister Peggy, to pour tea instead. For the first time since she had entered the convent after the war, Peggy was travelling on her own, unaccompanied by another Sister of Saint Joseph, and she was able to stay at her family's home and not in the convent on the Ontario side of the Ottawa River. For the last five years, Sister Peggy had been the nursing supervisor of the emergency department at Saint Vincent's in Greenwich Village. Verna had every confidence her sister-in-law could find her way to Saint Columba.

Verna knew how to entertain and how to throw an elegant do, but she was nervous about her sister-in-law's visit, because Sister Peggy, who had always been quite haughty in Verna's presence and somewhat possessive of Verna's husband, had asked for an afternoon alone with her.

Verna heard the blast of the ferry horn and she drove to the dock where Sister Peg would be dropped off. Ice remained on the river, but it was clear enough for the ferry to cross. They disagreed on much, she and the good sister, though her husband – a man of great integrity and goodness – treated his sister with the utmost respect. It drove Verna Dingle mad.

Sister Peggy had nursed overseas during the war. She was, by all reports, a woman who enjoyed all the pleasures of life, and her family was dismayed when she announced she was entering the covenant.

The last time she had visited Saint Columba, Peggy wore her imposing black habit, went by her religious name, Sister Saint Phillip, travelled with another sister, and stayed at a convent located on the other side of the river. Verna and Aloysius had visited her in New York, but Peggy had not seen any of her nieces or nephews for five years.

Verna was determined to treat Peggy like everyone else, but felt she was waiting for royalty at the dock. When Verna saw Peggy, she thought of the Irish who had come to Canada during the famine. Sister Peggy was emaciated. Her hair was thinning, most likely from years of wearing a veil. At forty-four, she looked forlorn and impoverished.

Verna had always taken great pleasure in trying to knock Sister Saint Phillip off her high horse. She had always found her to be the coldest of any of her husband's family.

"Sister Peg, how much money have you made for that convent of yours over the years? Would it kill them to buy you a decent suit and pay for a good hair cut? You look terrible."

Sister Peg extended her hand and said, "I'm grateful you came to pick me up on your own."

"I told a white lie and said you are arriving tomorrow. Aloysius is, of course, officiating at the parade on Sunday. I'm a tad concerned because Don Messer is playing at the arena and of course Al could wind up drinking with him. The kids are at their grandmother's house."

Verna carried her sister-in-law's bag to the car and they drove through Saint Columba to the new house – located on the Ottawa River on the edge of town – that had been recently completed.

"This house belongs on a ravine in Rosedale, Verna, not in this village. Not Rosedale, because the place is too modern and cold. It's an insult to the other homes. What were you thinking?"

"I am thinking we need a house lady to help out. Not me, Sister Peg. Your brother wants to lord it over everyone. With Al gone all week and me alone with the kids, it is too much.

"Your mother is eighty-four and still crazy. I think she's happy to be living in her own home with the pine trees, the river, and just being able to go outside whenever she wants. She gives mass in the privacy of her living room with the kids as her celebrants. They think she's great fun. The stories she tells them frighten them. The ghost stories. But I believe it's a good thing to frighten children with stories from the other side. It prepares them in life for the road ahead."

"How ridiculous, Verna. But your children are afraid of me too?"

"Yes. They don't know you. Like their grandmother, they think you are a witch. Aloysius employed a girl to look after your mamma. Her name is Jackie and she's a knockout. Mamma had to show her how to fry bacon and eggs because Jackie can't cook to save her life. Your mother might be schizophrenic, but she knows her way around a kitchen. The kids love Jackie and the boys in town think she's Jean Shrimpton."

"I'll try to visit mother while I'm in Saint Columba. But time is dear." Sister Peg opened her black purse, took out a bottle of holy water and sprinkled it around Verna's kitchen. She shut her eyes and silently prayed.

There wasn't time to defend herself against silent accusatory prayers and Verna chose to not comment on her sister-in-law's action. Sister Peg was a guest in her home and Verna would wait until she drove to the ferry when she was leaving before she would comment on her visit.

"All right, I have lots of wine and don't need to get groceries. But you need to help me make this bloody soda bread. I guess you'll want tea, not wine. We need to make twelve loaves to serve after the Saint Patrick's Day play, and to get through that I need Zing. I want you to write a review of the play for the *Saint*

Columba Times. It might seem too secular for you. There is no honesty allowed. Only good notices for the three performers. An endorsement from the good sister of Saint Joseph who lives in New York would serve us well."

"What play are you producing this year? I will have a little wine, thank you."

"Waiting for Godot. But you can't tell anyone. We are billing it as a surprise show."

"Beckett in Saint Columba. Have you lost your mind?"

"But no. How much more could I take of *My Sister Eileen* or *I Remember Mama*? Beckett is Irish. He would like it that we cast three women."

"Is he Catholic?"

"Not an Orangeman, anyway."

Sister Peggy stood in the large kitchen. An architect had been employed to design the house that was built to fit in with the property as if it were part of the landscape. A sunken living room, a large kitchen with a table and benches, a dining room that was a floor lower than the kitchen. The second floor was an office for Aloysius and master bedroom with a bathroom off it; on the third there were five bedrooms.

"How many bathrooms are in this house?"

"Four. You've yet to see the downstairs, which has an enormous family room where the kids can play billiards and ping pong and stay out of our hair."

The living room faced into the backyard with a view of the Ottawa River and Oiseaux Rock, which had once been a native sacred place. Peggy recalled boating to the rock and hiking to the top with her sister and brother when they were younger, when they only had a double-seater outhouse to use in the summer and winter. They kept a pot under the bed to pee in during the night.

Peggy put her leather suitcase in the bedroom and felt uneasy in this grand home. Her brother and his wife had once lived in one of the twenty wartime houses in Saint Columba. But that was before Aloysius had gone to law school and charmed himself into becoming a prosecutor for the county. During the week he mostly stayed on the Ontario side of the river in the seat of the county.

Like many of his crowd he drank to excess. Her brother was a man on his way to disaster with his easy laugh, a clever wit, and tendency to take the easier road.

Sister Peggy shuddered when she remembered she would most likely have to visit her mother, but this evening would be too busy. Her mother was always a little less open to the voices she heard in the morning light. They did not speak, she and her mother. It had been so long since Peggy had breathed a word to her mother she would not know where to begin.

When they were together, Peggy's mother spoke to the voices, but not to her. Sister Peggy would sit on a chair in the corner of the room and say the rosary over and over and her mother often thought she was a witch.

Verna put the fear of God in her kids before Sister Peggy's visit. She told them that their aunt from New York City would scorn and shame them if they acted like country children who left wet towels on the floor.

Verna demanded their kids do the chores around the house and they knew to wash the cutlery first, how to make a proper corner on a bed, and that one cleans from the top of the house down.

Sister Peg changed into her pajamas and Viyella robe. Both had been a present from Verna and Aloysius. She said," I am grateful for the comfort of this robe. I have a little present for you too, Verna."

Verna winced in anticipation of a bottle of holy water from Saint Patrick's Cathedral, or a rosary blessed by the Pope, and was taken aback when Sister Peg handed her a copy of *Django Reinhardt and the Hot Club Quintet.*

"The world is upside down. Jazz. Sister Peg, what in God's name is going on?"

"A patient gave it to me.

"The last time I was here, at the tea you held for me, Grace asked if I ate ice cream cones and what I wore to go swimming. Grace was shocked when I told her I wore a bathing suit. Her hands shook when she gave me a cup of tea."

Verna mixed a batch of whole-wheat flour, baking soda, buttermilk and salt. Expertly, without measuring, she mixed it in an enormous bowl while she sipped on a mug of wine.

"Grace thought you were a witch and she'll faint when she sees you in PJ's. They are all older now and not as stupid."

Verna Dingle had been eager to share her news with her sister-in-law, whom she enjoyed shocking.

"The cross on the bread will keep away the devil," said Verna. "Have you met any Catholic women who are taking the Pill? You must have at the hospital. When I was in confession, I asked about it. Couldn't believe my ears when the priest told me to go ahead and take the Pill but not to tell anyone. I am taking it. I have not told anyone, but I can tell you because you are so close to God."

Verna smiled and waited for her sister-in-law to argue with her as if she was the devil.

Sister Peggy opened the oven door and said, "Verna, you forgot to turn on the oven or are you cooking in a pan on the stove? Who am I to question a priest? I'm just a servant of the Lord."

Verna turned on the oven with one hand and with the other touched Peggy's arm and said, "Do I detect sarcasm? Of course you loathe it that I'm taking the Pill, with the priest's – and, I might add, your brother's – blessing."

Sister Peggy moved to the kitchen table and took a sip of her wine and said, "Children are God's gift to us. If I were the priest I would have said no. I also hate it that women are not allowed in the priesthood."

Verna ate a spoonful of raw soda bread from the bowl and said, "I should feed you. I'm stunned."

"It has become very strained living at the convent. I don't want to live there anymore."

"Now who has lost her mind? You're a nun. You can't decide where to live."

"Do you ever regret leaving Ireland to marry my brother?"

"Sister Peg. Are you drunk?"

Verna opened the fridge and took out some ham, bread, butter and mustard to make sandwiches.

Sister Peggy blessed herself and turned away.

"Verna, when I leave here I am going to the Madonna House in Combermere for a month to pray for discernment over whether or not I should leave the order."

As she buttered the bread, Verna said, "They don't have proper plumbing at the Madonna House. You silly goose, that is no place for you. If it's any consolation to you, I have sisters in Ireland with kids I haven't met yet. Grace talks about her aunt the nun who lives in New York City all the time. Maybe you should leave the convent, but you can't come home any more than I can go back to live in Dublin. Are you drinking more wine?"

"Yes, I am and what of it? Aloysius says you would rather fight than eat, Verna. And I would, too. Rather fight than eat but I can only hide behind my prayers. But not at work where they call me Sister A Bitch behind my back. It is prideful but I secretly adore my nickname."

Verna was delighted and said, " Yes, how tiresome it must be to a goody two-shoes. When it's cooled, pack up some soda bread to take to your mother's in the morning. I can make more. Discern while you stay with your mamma for the month. Talk to her. Listen to her voices. You might be surprised."

Sister Peg lay down on the couch in the kitchen and by the time the Irish soda bread was done, she was asleep.

Elvis was Dead

Julie believed that she deserved a man who would do sex on her. She was bored with her husband Gordon. On their wedding night the mattress fell through the springs and Gordon was her cowboy. He laughed and said, "Honey, the hardest part is paying my fees."

It was something he overheard a bronco rider say at the rodeo.

Julie said, "Let's do it again. I am smart and beautiful."

After their honeymoon things changed. Gordon would only feel her breast through her white cotton nightie while he watched television.

Julie would say, "Be a man, not a duck." But it didn't help.

Julie knew that she counted for something because she was born on the eighth of January. Everyone knew that Elvis Presley was born on the same day as Julie. Whenever she had a birthday, there were two cakes. It didn't matter to her that she was a few years younger than Elvis. She couldn't count and had to rely on Gordon to put the candles on the cakes. Even though he understood that the second cake wasn't really for Elvis, Gordon felt Julie was a run around girl.

It frightened Julie that her husband had guessed the truth. She liked to imagine she belonged to Elvis. She was afraid to ask Gordon to try some of the things she thought about and longed to know if they were possible.

Gordon convinced her to quit her job at the workshop and to leave the Strathcona Chippers, her bowling team. Julie missed her friends.

Gordon told her that even Priscilla Presley stayed at home to look after her husband.

Julie said, "Elvis isn't hers now. Don't even say her name."

Gordon told Julie that real wives have babies.

She said, "Your mother stuck you in Red Deer. That's what she did with her baby."

"My mother had to put me there. She didn't want to. You care more about your bowling team than you do about me."

He left to go out for a submarine at a strip joint and Julie put Elvis on their eight-track.

That night they ate their tuna fish casserole in silence. After dinner they argued over who would do the dishes. Gordon cried while he watched a rerun of *Rawhide* and Julie left the dirty plates and pots in the sink.

"It's not fair that I can't put on Elvis when you're here. I hate Del Shannon. I'm sick of this, Gordon. I want a job. I want to go back to the Chippers and I want you to do sex on me. The government doesn't care if we have fun. They just won't let us have babies. It isn't my fault, Gordon. They just did it."

Gordon turned off the TV. "I held your hand when we saw Sweet Daddy Siki."

Julie stomped her foot. "Big deal."

Gordon said, "No baby. No sex. That's the way it works."

Julie said, "You aren't the boss of me. Anyway. I was fixed. You know that."

Gordon scared her sometimes. He knew all the bus routes by heart and memorized the words to songs without even thinking about it. The staff wanted him to learn how to fix pianos because he had such a good ear. But Julie had to remind him to take his medication for his epilepsy and he needed help cooking Kraft Dinner. She believed that Gordon had too many bus routes and too many songs in his head.

She tossed and turned and imagined Gordon dying in a fire after he had a seizure while he was trying to make Kraft Dinner.

She reminded herself that Gordon was the reason she was unhappy. Julie was afraid that without him she would have to go back to a group home.

Julie had grown up in an institution in Red Deer. One Sunday night in 1956, Gordon sat beside her in the recreation hall while they watched Elvis for the first time on television. After the show, Julie said, "That boy Elvis is a dreamboat and so are you."

She told Gordon that she lived in Red Deer because the nurse crossed her mother's legs and stole half her brain. The doctor was busy and Julie tried to come along too soon. Gordon called Julie "Early Bird."

She said, "I wasn't early. The doctor was late."

Gordon smiled and sang "Hound Dog." He knew all the words. They became boyfriend and girlfriend that night.

The staff said that people like her and Gordon now belonged in the real normal world. By then Julie was listening to Elvis singing from Vegas. Julie and Gordon left the institution in 1975 to live in a group home in Edmonton. A year later Julie's dream came true. She and Gordon were married by a justice of the peace. Gordon had his hair cut like David Cassidy's. Julie wore a white lace Indian cotton dress she bought at Fairweather with her staff discount.

After their honeymoon, Gordon told her that they may as well shoot themselves.

"Being a husband is hard cheese to swallow. My father told me all about it."

"A staff comes by the apartment once a week to help us out. Let her worry over the bills, Gordon."

Julie's husband stopped making fun of his father and singing on buses.

When they got married, the *Edmonton Journal* ran a story on Julie and Gordon and gave them a year's subscription as a wedding present. Julie and Gordon liked to joke that they were stars because they did their own laundry. On their wedding day,

Julie had carried a pot of mums. She and Gordon knew that the mums would get a laugh or two when she threw the bouquet. Gordon told her he was sorry for reading the part that said the potted mums added an adorable touch to the ceremony. Gordon told her not to fret and to remember that reporters aren't funny guys.

The newspaper was delivered every morning to their apartment door. Gordon enjoyed reading the paper over breakfast and he was worried about what would happen in October when their subscription ran out. Julie believed that Gordon was trying to act like his father. She liked to listen to the radio and was pleased when she turned to a station that was playing "Heartbreak Hotel."

After the song, the announcer said, "Elvis Aaron Presley: dead at forty-two."

Gordon was hidden behind the newspaper while he ate a bowl of Cheerios.

He said, "It's true. I didn't want to tell you."

"Now it's too late to go to Graceland," she said.

Gordon said, "I'm glad he's dead."

Julie said, "That's it. It's vamoose to you. Hope the horses kick you."

Gordon left to go to the race track where he cleaned stalls as a volunteer.

Julie put her bowling shoes into an overnight bag. She left the apartment and walked up the hill to Jasper Avenue. She went into the lobby of the MacDonald Hotel and sat in one of the leather chairs. Julie was grateful for the t-shirt Gordon had bought for her during Klondike Days. It was important to Julie to not look out of place. There was an image of wild horses on the shirt. Gordon's dream was to ride a mustang bareback and Julie was certain that most of the people in the lobby owned a herd or two. Once Gordon had told her she was better than any horse running around the foothills. She was sorry that now she and Gordon had suspicious minds.

As she was leaving the hotel, the concierge pointed to the buttons attached to her t-shirt and said, "Too bad about Elvis."

Julie said, "He should've have chewed his food. I still have my eight-tracks."

She walked to the bowling alley but it was closed. Julie realized she was hungry and thought about going back to the apartment. Instead, she walked into a restaurant and sat down. Julie tried to remember what Gordon did when they went out for supper.

The man behind the counter said, "There's no table service. What will it be?"

She walked to the counter, pretended to read the menu on the wall and said, "A cheeseburger, chips and gravy, and a large coke."

Gordon told her that a five-dollar bill is enough to pay for almost anything. She took the money out of her wallet and said, "Too bad about Elvis, isn't it?"

As he handed her the change he said, "Someday, those buttons will be worth money."

Julie was enjoying herself. She ate her cheeseburger and was pleased that she knew how to chew without dying. She hoped that her curse on Gordon had not come true and that he wasn't kicked at work. It was too bad that Gordon was afraid to ride a horse.

She wondered who would look after Gordon now that she was gone. Priscilla dumped Elvis and she was known as a fat-assed bitch. But she probably had her own apartment. When Elvis was alive he was strong. But Elvis was dead. Julie decided Gordon could keep her eight-tracks.

The man behind the counter looked in Julie's direction. She suspected that he wanted her.

Hush Puppies

My family owned a garage located on Highway 17 and when I worked on Saturdays taking the cash I envied the woman in a torn picture that hung on the washroom wall. She was blonde, long-legged and beautiful. She stood in a stream, with a white lace nightgown pulled over her hips. The lace strap fell from her shoulder. She gazed lovingly at a man standing on the shore who held a fishing rod in his hand. She was peeing in the water and he was clearly enchanted by her beauty, her limbs, her cleavage, her ivory skin and her white pure piss.

In my heart I wanted enchantment. And I knew I would have to move further west along Highway 17. I wanted to find a place where no guy would howl at the moon when I made him come with my hand in the back seat of a car at the quarry.

I answered an ad in the Mackay Nugget for a waitress at the staff cafeteria in Deep River. It was fifty miles west of the garage and Mackay High. Collins and Collins hired me and offered to put me up at the staff hotel. There was a shoe store in Deep River but during the two months I spent there no one called me "Hound Dog."

Many of the inhabitants of Deep River worked at the nearby nuclear research centre. Some were scientists. Some were technicians. University students were hired from across the country to work at the centre for the summer and they stayed at the staff hotel. I was the only woman living in the building. I saw the ratio as a great opportunity to be redeemed.

The cook from the cafeteria, who was a thin, religious, gay man, the dishwasher who was on parole from Millhaven, and I were the only locals living at the hotel. Of the three of us, I had the most education. I had graduated from Grade 12. Fifty male students from places such as Vancouver occupied the other rooms.

The medical student from Nova Scotia who asked me to go sailing on a Sunday afternoon did not know how to respond when I was unable to say a word. He asked if I was chilly on a hot, humid day. I froze when he looked at my face. The math major from Winnipeg asked me to pick blueberries with him; my head and hands shook and I was not able to touch the bush.

When Harvey sat beside me on the beach while I was sunbathing on my break I felt at home. He was interested in medieval archiving and was nearing completion of his master's in library science from U of T. I resented him for not being the medical student from Nova Scotia or the math major from Manitoba.

Harvey was dressed in pants and a long-sleeved shirt and he held a large rock in his hand. He told me he was afraid of the locals and wanted to protect himself. When I took the towel off my stomach he noticed an enormous blister from my sunburn and asked if he could burst the white bubble that covered my midriff. I poured more olive oil over the blister and told him I felt healthier when I had a tan. Harvey did not touch me and I did not answer his question.

He talked about medieval poetry and Dante and said he had never exposed his body to the sun. I said, "Dante or you?"

"Both."

Enchantment was eluding me. I decided to go on a water fast to rid myself of toxins and to lose weight. For ten days I drank black coffee, diet pop and water. When the math major from Winnipeg came through the lineup at the cafeteria, I felt disdainful because he needed food to survive.

Harvey asked me to go shoe shopping with him. I had gone sailing and picked blueberries with two fine guys. I did not need to eat. I was tanned. I was lean.

Harvey carried his rock while we walked along the tree-lined street from the staff hotel to the shoe store. I told him there weren't many locals living in Deep River. He had nothing to worry about. I knew that a little further east Harvey might stir violence in the heart of an Ottawa Valley guy.

Harvey bought twelve pairs of matching Hush Puppies. He told me that he needed a few pairs of shoes because when one pair betrayed him he could rely on the next. I wanted to celebrate and invited Harvey to lunch. It was the first time Harvey had walked into a draft room. We sat on the Ladies and Escorts side and Harvey was anxious over who might be on the Men's side of the room. I broke my fast with a pickled egg and a draft.

That night, my laundry disappeared from the dryer. None of the men in the building could fit into my size twenty-eight jeans. Since I had cleansed my system, they were no longer tight enough to wear. But I wanted my underwear and was left with only my shabby laundry-day undies. I didn't know who had walked off with my clothes, but I suspected it was Harvey.

The cook lent me a pair of jeans and the dishwasher gave me three black T-shirts.

I told Harvey that at the turn of the century a headless skeleton was found near the river. The guy was never identified and his head was never found. It was believed he was a man passing though, most likely a lumberjack working in the area for the summer. I told him that the locals do not take well to someone from out of the area getting crushes on their women.

Harvey said, "I want to give you my mother's silver. In my home we dressed for dinner every night. The table was set with silver cutlery and it is what I most remember about growing up. A linen tablecloth and silver cutlery. I want you to have the silver."

"Just one piece," I said.

Harvey went home to Montreal for the weekend and for me it was an enormous relief. Every night, he had dropped by my room, and I started to run to the river and hide behind the pine trees. I sensed that Harvey wanted to ask me out and he simply could not do it.

On Sunday night, it was calm outside after a rainstorm and then there was a mighty wind. I was working late at the cafeteria. And the cook and dishwasher were gone. The guy who I went blueberry picking with walked into the kitchen. He told me there was a tornado warning and we should go to the basement. Surrounded by grey concrete walls while trees and cars got knocked over outside he ripped the collar off my uniform that belonged to Collins and Collins and slapped my face while I cried and said, "I'm not really like that."

The tornado passed and we went upstairs. I walked to the staff hotel carrying my last pair of underwear in my hand, with blood streaming from my mouth.

Harvey came by when he returned and knocked at my door but I did not breathe and he left. I put on the cook and dishwasher's clothes and walked to the river. It was a magnificent night. I took off the jeans and t-shirt and went into the dark water. I liked the feel of pieces of bark touching my feet and the sand at the bottom of the river between my toes. I swam in the choppy water and for a while forgot about the tornado. Pine tree branches floated around my body.

I swam to shore and walked on the beach towards my clothes and I saw Harvey sitting on a log. There was not a sound from him or his feet. I stood still for a second and felt as though I was the woman in the photo at the garage. Harvey did not hold a fishing rod in his hands but he was enchanted. I wished I had peed in the water before I came to shore but I was already standing on the ground. I got dressed while Harvey watched. Then I turned and walked to the staff hotel alone on the road while Harvey followed behind.

A silver serving spoon with a white mother of pearl handle arrived at my parents' garage and they forwarded it to me where I was living further west on Highway 17.

Further west than Deep River.

Bareback

Maryanne wanted to reclaim her virginity and to be born again. She registered in a course for adults who wanted to convert to Catholicism. At the first class, Maryanne was suitably dressed in a red sweat suit. The universe wanted her to be naked in her spirituality and to not muddy the waters with fashion.

The priest who greeted the twelve students asked them to move their chairs away from their desks and sit in a semicircle.

"The Roman Catholic Church is the living body of Jesus Christ on Earth. Many of you must have a thirst for God, some have been coerced into coming here by a prospective spouse eager to marry in the church, or the hound of heaven has been biting your heels. What brought you to Saint Peter's doesn't matter. All that matters is that you are here. Maybe you are a lapsed – what we used to call a 'fallen' – Catholic, who wants to renew his or her faith."

Maryanne raised her hand and nodded in acknowledgment of her fallen status.

"Please, introduce yourself and feel free to talk about your relationship with the Church."

"My name is Maryanne Brennan. A couple of years ago I came into recovery. I was so sick when I came into the program. It helped me a lot, but now I need more than the twelve steps.

"I want to meet a like-minded man. Excuse me: like-minded people. I'm here because I want to know more about how I can allow Jesus to be my lover.

"I was raised Catholic, but know little about the true traditions of the Church. As a child, part of being a Catholic for me was going to the annual Knights of Columbus Christmas party. One year, Santa was drunk. He fell when he was running up the aisle and broke his nose. There was blood on his beard and the smell of booze on his breath, but he still gave out the candies. Jesus, God the father and the Holy Spirit were present that afternoon."

"You're in the right place, Maryanne. By the end of these twelve weeks, you'll have more of an understanding of the Living Church."

The man sitting beside Maryanne was wearing work boots that seemed too large for his feet and he desperately needed a haircut. There was something intriguing about this scruffy guy who drew a picture of the grim reaper on his arm while the others shared about themselves. He was the last person to speak.

"You can call me Nelson. My last name is Orr. I do not come from a religious background, but in my heart I am a Catholic. My image of God is Mohammed Ali. He hangs out on the ropes and when you are down he comes in swinging. You're his and there's dick all you can do about it. The crucifixion and the resurrection have always compelled me. Man, how I want to be redeemed. But it concerns me that Christ struck down the fig tree. It was such an irrational act."

"Yes. It's an enigma. Great theologians have debated the parable. Read what's been written and decide for yourself," the priest said.

"I already have," Nelson said.

Maryanne frowned and wanted to ask him if he had ever boxed.

The following week the subject was revelation and the Old Testament. Nelson told the priest that he'd read the Book of Job three times over the last year. Maryanne offfered that during that week she'd read the parable of the fig tree.

During the coffee break, Nelson shook Maryanne's hand.

"I'm a junkie. Does this mean I'm one of the like-minded people you're seeking out?"

"I don't know."

"What twelve-step program are you in?"

"Sex and Love Addicts Anonymous. S.L.A.A. I have nothing to be ashamed of. It's an illness too," Maryanne said.

"I like the way you wear your hair, Maryanne. I've always been partial to a sporting look."

"Heh, Nelson, this is my take on the fig tree. It was just doing what a fig tree does. There's nothing wrong with that, but Jesus was tired and hungry. He was God and he was a guy, too. Maybe that's it. The guy part of God took over. Zapping things. Just because they are there."

Nelson told her that he was clean but still sinned.

"How've you stayed off heroin?" Maryanne asked.

"God and fucking. It's been twenty-six months since I stuck a needle in my arm. I pray and have sex whenever I can."

Maryanne made a mental note that this man was trying to get a rise out of her and she chose not to comment on his method of staying clean.

"I'm reading *Keys to the Kingdom*. Are you reading anything these days?" Maryanne asked.

"*A Walk on the Wild Side*. The break is over; let's pick this up after class."

"Sorry, I have to run," Maryanne said.

"Next week, then," said Nelson. "Be good."

Maryanne was grateful for the mushrooms that were growing between the cracks of tiles in her bathroom. Any day the bathroom might crash into the basement below. She could not invite Nelson over. He might be killed. After prevaricating for an hour, she dialed Nelson's home number.

"Good to hear from you. How did you get my number?"

"It was on the list of students handed out at the class."

"That was a mistake. I was very clear to those fuckers not to put my number on the list."

"Is it too late to call? What time do you have to get up in the morning?"

"I don't."

"What do you do?" she asked.

"I'm an unskilled labourer and a photographer. My work isn't for everyone. I haven't made a plugged nickel. I'm not an artiste. Someone who waits up all night to see the sunrise. I'm the kind of guy who would drive to Edmonton for a beer. If I had my license."

"You're a guy and you don't drive. That's impressive."

"Maryanne, I don't have a bank account or any ID. My dream is to get a passport and leave this fucking country. Canada is a sanitarium. A place to rest and recuperate. I want to live in Israel. Someday I will. How impressed are you now?"

"How did you get into photography? You don't seem the type."

"I was staying at a warehouse in Montreal. A friend let me spend a few nights in his storeroom. I was in love with this woman. Man she drove me nuts. I wanted to see her ass. I drew it. There was a camera in the office. I took a picture of the drawing. And when I finally had the film developed I wanted to make more. But of real women. When I take a picture, I want the observer to be able to smell her feet. That's how I got started. The drive to find one more train to rob sends me back to the camera. Bring back a woman's tears and move on. And it's time now to get out of here. Maybe next week we could go for a coffee and you can tell me more about yourself. All I really know about you is that you are wired to sex. If I knew you better, I'd say wired to coming. And now you want Jesus to be your lover."

"Don't make fun of me. At the end, sex was for me was pain and humiliation. It's hard for me to believe I am the same woman."

"Why did you call me?"

"Do you know anything about plumbing?"

Maryanne spent the weekend combing secondhand bookstores, looking for a copy of Nelson's book. She found one.

There were photos of women tied to radiators, women dressed in leather, and a shot of Nelson's head with a foot in his mouth. The last photo was of an ass with Nelson's name tattooed on the left cheek. Nelson was described as an uncircumcised man with big feet.

Maryanne was a bit concerned.

On her way to the third class, she ran into Nelson at Mac's Milk. He offered to buy her a muffin.

"I can buy my own muffin, thank you."

"That's the best part of sex for me," Nelson said. "Acting out."

They walked to Saint Peter's and Maryanne thought of the photo of a woman straddling a footstool with a big foot on her butt. Maryanne sensed that she could help Nelson. She needed to be prudent.

She did not tell Nelson that she had gone to eight bookstores before she found a copy of his book. She prayed for Nelson and decided he would be embarrassed if he knew she had a copy in her purse.

At class, the priest discussed the Trinity. Nelson walked Maryanne home afterwards. He hummed, "I told Mary about us.", before he kissed her on the cheek and said goodnight.

As he walked away, Nelson said, "That habit of yours is a killer."

At her weekly Sex and Love Addicts Anonymous meeting Maryanne talked about her sexual attraction to Nelson. Her sponsor told her it was old behaviour and to try to spend time with men who were emotionally available.

Maryanne went out with a man who worked for the Ministry of Agriculture in the egg department. He arrived at her apartment with a bouquet of carnations in his hand.

"Maryanne, I'm having digestive difficulties and am a little constipated. Would you mind if we just ordered in Chinese?"

While he was on the phone to a take-out place, Maryanne took Nelson's book into the washroom and imagined her ass being tattooed while Nelson watched.

Maryanne went back into the living room and said to her date, "I'm sorry. You have to leave. My bathroom isn't safe."

The next night, Maryanne ran into Nelson at the turnstile at the Eglinton subway. He still needed a haircut, his work boots were still too big, and he looked as though he was on his way from one bed to another.

"I broke up with my girlfriend. Now you and I can date."

"What girlfriend?"

"I get a little of this. A little of that. She was my main squeeze. Let's take in *A Passage to India*."

"It's a bad idea."

"Let's grab a coffee and talk things over," he said.

They each ordered a coffee and a sour cream doughnut. As Nelson paid the cashier, Maryanne noticed a mouse scampering over the doughnuts on the shelf. She nudged Nelson and said, "It's a bad omen. Let's get out of here."

Nelson decided to see *Blood Simple* for the second time and Maryanne lied and said she was meeting a friend.

That night, Maryanne read the literature from Sex and Love Addicts Anonymous. By the letter of the law, sex with Nelson would not be a slip. She said the Jesus Prayer.

She imagined sitting in a log cabin with only a picnic table in the room, and Jesus. On the picnic table there were no cups. Maryanne wondered if this meant she had not let the Lord into her heart.

"No insult to you, but Nelson needs a twelve-step program to stop running. Jesus, you can do it. Make him stop with 'a little of this and a little of that.' Fucking anything that moves. So that I can be with him. For just one night. Thank you Lord for healing Nelson."

Prayer, the church as a sacrament and the communion of Saints, baptism and the Eucharist were discussed as the weeks passed.

In May, the feast month of the Virgin Mary, Nelson and Maryanne went out for a hot dog after class and sat on the steps of the museum.

"God," Maryanne said, "I hate it when anyone asks what I do. I don't like what I do and I don't like what people think of what I do. I work in the service industry. I have wanted to quit for ten years. Since the day I started."

"Are you a hooker?"

"Please. I work at the downtown Y as an attendant. Handing out towels for a living isn't so bad. I think God is preparing me for something. Something more. He doesn't want me to be too distracted with passion or a job I love. He wants me to be waiting in joyful hope."

"Quit your job and grow your hair," Nelson said.

"I thought you liked my sporting look?"

"I was flirting. Why do you dress as though you're on a broomball team?"

"Where do you get off saying this stuff, Nelson?"

"Frankly, it irritates me that you are posing as a nun. But yes. I was out of line."

"You, of course, were a babe magnet in high school."

"I was a bookish guy who wanted to be a contender. In Grade 9, I took shop. But they told me to go back to reading books. I couldn't build anything. So I took up boxing. I used to sit in the cafeteria alone reading a book. When I beat a guy up over lunch hour, I got noticed. After school that day, a girl, Laura, took off her clothes for me under the stands in the football field. The next day, I quit school and stopped boxing. I didn't need it anymore. I gave them something to remember me by.

"I hitchhiked from Montreal to California and sent my parents a postcard. They were glad to be rid of me," Nelson said.

"Some guys I hung out with in high school nominated me as football queen. As a joke."

"Trying to cheer me up?" Nelson said. "Fucking cretins."

"Did things get better with your parents, Nelson?"

"Yes. My mother had a stroke last year and I visit her and my father when I can. It's strange. My mother loathes Catholics. But she's glad I want to convert."

"Have you ever used a gun?"

"Moving right along. Done with the family. On to weapons."

"Well?"

"Yes. I have. I tried to rob a greasy spoon I frequented in Vancouver. I took a pistol from a guy I knew on the street. The owner of the restaurant laughed when I pulled out the gun and told him to open his cash register. I just stood there for a bit, then said, 'How about a coffee and a burger?'

"He told me to pay first and to put away the gun.

"I put the gun in my pocket and walked out of the place. The guy didn't call the cops."

"I left home on a whim too, Nelson.

"The summer before Grade 13, I spent the night on the beach with a long-haired barefooted guy. We drank a couple of bottles of crackling rosé and had a wondrous night. The next time I saw him, he gave me a copy of *Highway 61 Revisited* and I told him it was time for me to leave Cow Shit Valley.

"I drank a bottle of Southern Comfort in Pansy Patch Park. Before the night was over I knew that I was leaving town the next day. In the morning I left for Manitoulin Island. I packed a picture of my father wearing a leather jacket and a fedora, standing with his buddies beside a fishing hut. He looked bad and beautiful.

"I have a good mind and a sense of humour. Those were gifts from my father. I don't have a talent for physics, but I too like poetry.

"I left a note for my mother and told her I was not coming back and that I was not going to get an education either. I told her I believed she would dance in the kitchen again and that her life would get better.

"I thanked her for not changing my last name when she married my stepfather. Then I left and spent a lot of years just fucking around."

"That's the story I want to hear," Nelson said. "You fucking around. Is your stepfather still alive?"

"My mother is religious, but she's practical, too. He was crawling around the house. My mother thought using a walker would take away from his dignity.

"When I told her to get him medical attention, she said, 'Maryanne, you don't understand. The doctor is dead.'"

"Their doctor had a heart attack around the time my stepfather's health started to fail. I explained to her that there were other doctors in town. She was determined to nurse him back to good health before she took him to see a physician.

"Before he was able to walk again, he died. My mother was right. He had sciatica but he also had high blood pressure."

Nelson laughed. "Your mother murdered your stepfather."

"Not really.

"When she called to tell me, she said, 'I've noticed that widows take out a new lease on life.' She did not ask me to attend the funeral and afterwards I visited the farm for the first time in years. Shortly after that my mother sold the place, moved into town, and joined an aerobics class. She kept herself in good shape, milking cows all those years. She put an ad in the local paper in the companions section. It read 'Lady seeks romance with man aged forty to eighty.' She had a lot of responses, but I don't know what came of any of them. She won't tell me. My mother is a love addict too."

"Like a trucker from Regina, let me maul you on Spadina. Don't you want a life, Maryanne? What's the point in reading the worst book ever written? Just because it won't put bad thoughts in your head. *Keys to the Kingdom*. Good God Almighty."

"It isn't the sex that scares me. It's what happens afterwards. You remind me too much of me. When I was sick and acting out."

Nelson put his hands on her shoulders. "It's you I want to know. And I need to fuck you."

"I bought your book. It's intriguing. I look at the pictures every night. Did you take them when you were still using drugs?"

"I'd like to take one of you handcuffed to a brass bed covered with shamrocks and thorns."

They went to the place Nelson was house-sitting. Maryanne paid the fare and Nelson carried her over the threshold.

"I haven't done any pre-sex stuff like shaving my legs."

"Pre-sex stuff turns me off."

He kissed her.

"Let's lie down on the couch, Maryanne."

"No, upstairs. In your bedroom."

They made love most of the night. A few blocks away, in Maryanne's apartment, there was a crashing sound. If Maryanne had been home she might have thought twelve men armed with baseball bats were having a row in her apartment. The floor had finally given in and crashed through to the moldy, musky, basement below Maryanne's place. Maryanne liked to believe it happened when she told Nelson she wanted to be his godmother.

At dawn they took the dog, Tiger, for a walk.

"Now I've gotten you out of my system."

"This wasn't just a jump in the hay. It's serious."

"I saw your whip. And felt sad."

"I don't know what the fuck you're talking about."

"It was over the rod in the bathroom."

"Maryanne, I'm dog sitting. That was Tiger's leash. Please don't make me fall out of love with you before breakfast."

"But Nelson, you're the first person I've had sex with in two years. I've things to do. A life to find, without a man."

"I'm not Picasso. I don't know why anyone sleeps with me. I'm a pauper and a burden."

"Must be all your funny stories."

"I want to fuck you in a ravine."

"After you convert?"

"Tonight, I'll come over to your place."

They looked at each other; he with his crooked grin and she with her eyes full of God took a breath.

"Bring Tiger's leash, Nelson."

Geography

"This morning, I sublet an apartment with a view of a big dumpster," Nelson told me. "The guy I leased the place from is taking off to California for a few months. He thinks someone is trying to kill him. Elastic bands are mysteriously showing up wrapped around the doorknobs and inside the kitchen cupboards."

"I thought you were moving in with me."

"Maryanne, once bitten twice shy. I don't trust you and know you could give me the boot on a moment's notice. You kicked me out before. It could happen again."

I told Nelson this was different because he was sick and that this time we had interferon to keep him faithful.

"I am not a cretin, Maryanne. It's all water under the bridge now and I forgive you for throwing me out in the rain. In Prague, Amsterdam or Liverpool, I will throw in my lot with you. Even in Greenland. I would rather be dead than live in Toronto. The sublet is a backup for us until we leave the country."

"Nelson, if you die, leave a message at the front desk. By then I'll be in a nursing home."

We hung up the phone. Nelson arrived by cab at midnight with his duffel bag, two cardboard boxes, his alto sax and his camera equipment. He had been taking music lessons in exchange for free photography.

While he carried his belongings upstairs, I told him that the cheapest place to live in Europe was Portugal. I told him I might go on without him and that he could meet me there in six months.

"That would be a frosty Friday," Nelson said.

At eight-thirty the next morning we were in the waiting room of Nelson's liver specialist at Mount Sinai Hospital. Nelson introduced me to Dr. Long.

"This is my partner," he said.

I was pleased with my official status, but concerned over what the specialist told us.

Dr. Long explained, "Hepatitis C is a slow-moving disease and you can look forward to at least ten good years. Unless you develop liver cancer or your cirrhosis worsens, which would kill you relatively quickly."

Afterwards, we went to the pharmacy in the lobby of hospital and, in exchange for a certified check for three thousand dollars, the pharmacist handed Nelson thirty-two bottles of interferon, a six-month supply of needles in plastic wrapping, and a container for contaminated syringes.

At the corner of University and College, Nelson gave a panhandler a two-dollar coin.

"That was my last cent. From now on, I'm nickel-and-diming it."

I gave Nelson a token to go home and he promised to pay for our move to Portugal.

At Saint Lucy's Co-op, where I lived, I was in charge of snow removal. On the condition that Nelson could choose the movie later at The Captain's Video, he agreed to help me. I noticed the palms of his hands were red before we bundled up to go outside. While we shoveled the snow, Nelson complained about living in a place that was so close to the train tracks.

I wanted to tell him that I already knew he would start up soon with another passing thing.

I wanted to tell him I was terrified I would wait for the passing thing to pass.

I wanted to tell him that leaving the country was a pipe dream.

The walkway and entrance remained treacherous even though Nelson had poured two bags of salt outside of Saint Lucy's Co-op. St. Lucy was the patron saint of eyes and we left it in her hands that no one would take a catastrophic fall.

Before we went to bed, we each read a few verses of the Book of Job.

Nelson told me he was afraid that once he started his treatments he would lose interest in sex.

Then he tied me to my brass bed and said, "Will you do anything for me?"

"Yes, if you do all the work."

Afterwards, he said, "Nighty-night, lamb of London."

With the wind howling outside, and already in a dream-like state, I fell asleep.

Nelson injected his first shot of interferon the next morning and I took the day off work. I vomited five times. Each time I said, "That was the last time. Turn the TV back on. I'm sorry. I'm supposed to be looking after you, Nelson."

Then I would run back upstairs. Nelson ate the Chinese take-out and voiced his regret over watching a silent movie.

At night, while we slept, the drug started to make Nelson sick. He broke into a cold sweat and was shivering and asked me to hold him.

"Nelson, I won't even buy a dog because it might die."

He fell asleep in my arms and slept the sleep of wolves until he woke up in a panic at four a.m.

He went downstairs and attempted to play "A Groovy Kind of Love" on his sax. When he came back to bed, he seemed relieved.

"Honey-bunch, 'A Love Supreme' came to Coltrane in a dream and not long after that he died. 'A Groovy Kind of Love' came to me in a dream and that means I'm just another schmuck who dreams up a tune, wakes up, and thinks it's brilliant until he plays it and realizes he heard it on the radio a thousand times."

"Better a schmuck than a visit from God, Nelson."

In the morning my mother called from Saint Columba to inquire about Nelson, who she believed to be a man with a great sense of humour. She told me that taking care of Nelson was the best thing I had ever done in my life.

By the evening, he was much sicker and, when I came home from grocery shopping, he was lying in bed covered with quilts and blankets. The window was open and cold winter air was blowing into the bedroom.

"Where have you been? You need to shut the window."

"Working at the bookstore, working to make a dollar. You must have gotten up to pee. Why didn't you shut the window then?"

"I want you to do it."

As I closed the window, I said, "My mother rented *The Bad Lieutenant* and she says there is a kind of humour to it and good acting. Do you want to check it out?"

Nelson told me he was too ill to walk downstairs to watch a movie. I took off my clothes and crawled in beside him. He had a fever and his unshaven face was vaguely yellow. His body was warm and I told him I had something on my mind.

"What is it?"

"Twenty years ago I went to see Masie Davidson who told fortunes even though it was a sin in the eyes of the church. Masie would take the picture of the Sacred Heart off the kitchen wall and place it on her bedroom dresser before doing a reading. She told me that someone I love would die because of liver disease."

"Masie fucking Davidson. Maryanne, show a little sensitivity. I have a temperature of one hundred and five."

I explained to Nelson that Masie enjoyed giving morbid readings and that sometimes she lied.

Nelson pulled the quilt over his head and mumbled, "Let's make a deal. Don't tell me anymore stories about the Ottawa Valley and I won't fuck around while I am under your roof. Do tell me what else was in your cards. I'm itching to know."

"She said I would receive a letter."

"That's it?"

"Yes. That was all Masie saw in my reading."

"That's sad, Maryanne."

A strange sound came from beneath the store-bought quilt and I thought Nelson was laughing. Then I realized he was weeping.

When I was a Brownie, I was pulled into Guides because I could not quilt a square. My friends were flown into Guides and I was pulled with pink crepe paper. Nelson would not enter heaven on wings. I wished I could make him a quilt, a shroud, to cover him while he waited to be yanked into the great beyond.

"Can you imagine your funeral? When your three ex-wives each believe they were the one you loved the most. I wonder where I'll fit into it all?"

"You won't be there, Maryanne. I'm taking you with me."

"As much as I might like that, Nelson, you are on your own."

Nelson rolled over without saying goodnight and I thought about Masie Davidson and her reputation for giving accurate readings.

After three weeks he started to feel better, but still was not able to play his sax. Nelson noticed that he enjoyed the daily ritual of injecting a needle every morning and feeling ill most of the day. It reminded him of his other life.

At the library at Princess Margaret Hospital, I researched Nelson's disease.

I bought a bottle of milk thistle at the health food store and cooked meals that were low in fat. We rented two film noir movies a day and ate dinner during the first show. Nelson started going out during the day to buy a carton of cream and would hide the container before I got home.

Every time I spoke to my mother, she told me that taking care of Nelson was the best thing I'd ever done.

Nelson paid to have cable hooked up. For the first time in our relationship, we watched television together and ended most nights with *Studs*. I decided to cook with butter and cream.

The leather corset Nelson bought me at a shop near World's End when we were in London a couple of years before would no longer zipper and he was usually too tired to tie me to the bed. He told me my weight gain was off-putting and I lied and said that I found his added pounds erotic.

The redness on the palms of his hands was spreading and we stopped reading the Book of Job every night before going to bed. He told me I acted as though I were running an inn and each morning I had to get up to clean the stable. He said he felt like Flicker.

I wanted Nelson to believe in heaven. He did not.

It enraged him when I told him I missed going to listen to him play at the Bistro.

"You are the kind of woman who likes to be with a man who is smarter than her. Lots of women only want reflected glory. Don't worry, because I am taking you with me. Man, once they put us in the ground, that's the end of the story. So Maryanne, we have to get the fuck out of here."

"I simply won't have it. You can't die, Nelson."

I told him I needed to do snow removal.

Three months passed and my mother invited us to spend Easter in Saint Columba. I lied and told Nelson I had agreed to work at the bookstore. Feel free to go on your own, I told him. Like myself, he didn't give much credence to an old biddy, but he went because he wanted Masie Davidson to read his cards.

At the bus terminal, I kissed him goodbye and promised to arrive in Saint Columba on Tuesday.

Nelson took his duffel bags, his sax, and the remaining interferon. He left the two boxes in my storage closet.

He asked me to check the mail at his sublet.

"Beware of elastic bands," he said.

On Saturday, I sold the upright piano my grandmother left me to a neighbour for seven hundred dollars. At New Adventures Travel, I was told that my budget would allow me to purchase a ticket to Saskatoon. My flight was scheduled to leave in a week. I hid the ticket inside the King James Version of the Book of Job.

Nelson called from Saint Columba and said that Masie Davidson had been dead for years. I told him I was sorry that I hadn't known. Nelson's persuasive abilities were difficult for me to resist. I decided not to tell him my plans. I suggested that he stay with my mother for a couple of weeks and he said it was a great idea. I told him I would drop him a line, which I did do when I arrived in Saskatchewan.

In June, Nelson decided to continue to stay with my mother.

"I guess it's best to bury him here," my mother said.

Nelson made her laugh until the day he passed away.

I thanked my mother for taking care of him. I told her I only wanted his saxophone.

I imagined my mother standing in the kitchen by the telephone with a rhinestone barrette on the side of her dyed red flapper blunt hairstyle. At seventy-five, it was unlikely she had changed her style, and the image gave me a sense of unwavering constancy.

"Maryanne, don't be upset, but he asked me to keep it safe and sound in Saint Columba. He was worried that in a pinch you might pawn it."

I told my mother that Nelson was right.

That night, during my weekly gig playing keyboards at a club called White Dogs of Texas, I laughed out loud when I thought I saw Nelson sitting in a corner basking in the reflected glory of my rendition of "Every Time We Say Goodbye."

Of course, it wasn't him, because once they put you in the ground, man, that is the end of the story.

Wonderland

This morning, my roommate Annie Banana and me watched the comings and goings in the lobby on our TV set. The plan was to take Art's shuttle bus to the mall like we do every Friday. But when I got up from my lazy chair to get ready, I threw up all over the place. My roommate was fed up because I have been getting sick since Tuesday.

"Enough is enough." Annie picked up the phone and said, "I'm dialing a nine and a one and another one. My roommate, Doreen Logan, is sick. She needs help. Come right now to our building."

"Shut up, Annie. I'll get in trouble. Tell them it's not this Doreen Logan."

Then Annie called her sisters and the staff who told her she did the right thing because this is an emergency.

I told Annie she was scaring me and to not use that word. Emergency.

When the ambulance men came, I told them today is the day we take out one hundred dollars for our overnight to the Wonder Palace Casino at Niagara Falls. I put a scare in them when I said, "If you don't get me back here after lunch, Annie will get after you with a broom."

The ambulance man talks to Mighty Mouse on the phone and he says, "Oh they are retarded. I'm sorry. Developmentally handicapped."

I said to him, "That's not a nice thing to say about an apartment girl. We don't care about what word you use for us because we are smart. Don't use the R word, Mr. Man"

Lots of people in my apartment building go to the hospital by ambulance. It's faster, and I pretend I am on a show like *Ben Casey*.

I wonder out loud who'll clean up my chair and the rug.

I tell the ambulance man, "It's not my problem now. It's the damn staff's problem and Annie will have to put up with it. The staff always comes on Monday, but next week she is going with us to the Wonder Palace Casino in Niagara Falls. Me and Annie know how to act when we are on vacation. We've been apartment girls looking after ourselves for a long time now. We've flown away on a plane and have passports; that means we can go anywhere we want to. Yes, we can."

The ambulance man asks me to place a bet for him in Niagara Falls, but I tell him my roommate is the lucky one.

Mighty Mouse shows up at the hospital in the emergency room. She doesn't wear a hat in the rain, but she's not so bad. Her real name is Mary. She helped Annie and me move when that boy bled all over our hall rug.

Two years ago, a teenager got killed right outside our apartment door. Annie and I were eating spaghetti and there was a big bang sound and boom, blood was coming under our door. Annie put the chain lock on.

We could hear him saying, "Mother, mother, help me."

I looked through the peephole and said, "It's too late to call your mother, now. You should have thought of that earlier."

Annie telephoned her sisters and they said we should stay away from the door and to stay put in our apartment. They said someone else would call the police.

Annie and I didn't want to get blood on our slippers. There was no point in not doing our doings, so we finished our spaghetti. I did the dishes and then we watched the lobby on TV. There were policemen, the fire truck and two ambulances outside.

That's how we do our doings. Annie always cooks and I do the dishes and we mind our own business.

The police came and talked to us after that boy was taken away. He didn't live in our building and if he had stayed in his own home, none of this would have happened.

We already had our nightgowns and slippers on and they kept us up late. Annie played a nasty trick on the police and showed them all our pictures of our trip to Disneyland.

After that, Annie's sisters and the staff made us move. My family didn't say anything because I don't have one. Annie's family knows I've got no mother and that's why they treat me all the time.

My mother came to the Regional Centre for Retarded when I was a little girl and taught me how to knit on Popsicle sticks. I was born in a little town called Saint Columba, but I have never been there.

Before we met, Annie's parents died and her sisters were afraid she would have to live with them. I wanted to move into town from the Regional Centre and the staff at the Toronto office said Annie and I would be a good match. Like matchsticks. Get it?

Annie and I moved into our first apartment the year the Pope came to Toronto for the first time. I remember because the Bathurst bus was too filled for Annie and me to go to Honest Ed's on a Saturday morning. But we fooled the Pope and we moved just around the time that he came back to Toronto, and we don't take the Bathurst bus anymore. We take Art's shuttle bus or taxis. Don't look at me because I save my money. The office pays for us to go to town in a taxi because I have a bad knee.

Sometimes Annie calls her sister a blasted witch but never to her face. Sometimes she uses really bad words. Annie's sister yelled at us when we bought two singing fish to put on the wall. Annie's sisters and the staff tell us we don't need to buy two of everything and that we shouldn't dress the same. By rights, it's our money, and they should mind their own business. That's how we do our doings and that's too bad.

Now Annie and me are a couple of old chickens living at a senior's apartment building. Mighty Mouse got us in fast because of that boy that got blood all over our carpet. It wasn't our fault. Don't blame us. But it is better here anyways.

They have bingo and coffee every Wednesday morning. Annie always wins, even when she doesn't. At a Christmas party, I won a toque. I cried and said, "No, give it to Annie Banana because she's the lucky one. Not me." Annie's father gambled and he made plenty of money. Each time one of Annie's sisters got married, Annie's father gave her a diamond ring. Annie has so many she gave one to me. She likes me to win too. But if she doesn't win the same thing I am in big trouble.

When we go to the Wonder Palace Casino at Niagara Falls I like to buy things and go to the restaurant where they have a second plate of food. But lately I can't eat very much and I can't go number two. What am I going to do on Monday if I can't have a second plate of food at the Wonder Palace?

The doctor took a picture of my stomach and now he wants to stick a thing inside me down there and I said he was a crazy fool. I told him that's dirty and that someone hurt me there once. Mary Mighty Mouse tells me she'll hold my hand but the kill pain pill they give me sends me into a dream.

Now I am in a room with someone else sleeping in another bed. Breathing things are in my nose, my arm is tied down and I'll pull that needle out if I want to. Yes, I will. It's my arm. Mary Mighty Mouse tells me that just for tonight I can pee in bag and don't have to get up. I am hungry, my head is dizzy, and the nurses are rude.

Annie will be vexed if I don't come home tonight. Mary the staff is sitting in a chair and she looks like she has a sore neck. The nurse is playing with the drip in my arm and Mary says, "Doreen had a birthday party for herself two months ago. She rented the party room on the top floor of her co-op and invited all her friends. She was fine and just around that time she had her annual medical. Her doctor said she has the heart of a forty-year-old."

I am too tired to say that it isn't my heart that hurts.

When I wake up the next morning, Annie's sister and Mary are standing there just staring at me.

With my hand I point down there and say, "It hurts. I need a kill pain pill."

Annie's sister's hands remind me of home. Her fingernails are long, pretty and coloured red.

Every Sunday afternoon Annie does her nails and then she does mine. During the summer we have our toenails done at the mall. You see, we are different. I like pink and Annie likes red.

The staff tells me the Wonder Palace trip is cancelled. Our suitcases are packed with our Wonder Palace Niagara Falls clothes and the creams and soap we bought from the Avon lady. It'll keep until I get better and go home. The staff and Annie's sister don't know we buy things from the Avon lady.

The doctor comes in to talk to me and I don't know what he means. I think he said I was throwing up because I have a big ball in my stomach that they will take out so I can go number two again. Afterwards I might have to go number two in a plastic bag.

All of Annie's sisters are praying for me, even though I am not Catholic. Now I am really scared. I cry without making a sound and I didn't know I could cry without making a sound but I can.

Then I feel like I want to kick a can or a doorstop. I know why I am sick and I tell Annie's sister and Mary.

"Every Thursday night that Mark comes over to see Annie. His feet smell. He makes me sick. That's why I am sick. Smelling Mark's feet. He kisses Annie good, you know? I just knit my squares. Don't let him come to Niagara Falls because it's Mark's fault I am sick. That stupid guy he's always smiling. He's been coming over on Thursday nights for too long. Ever since the Pope's first visit, once a week, he comes into our apartment with his smelly feet. I want to talk to my roommate, Annie, right now."

They dial home for me and I ask Annie to lock my bedroom door and to not let Mark into my room because he steals pens. I tell Annie I'll be home soon. She tells me the super cleaned up my throw up and she has a card from Art the shuttle bus driver to give me.

Annie cries and tells me she's upset because her roommate Doreen Logan is in the hospital and we can't go to the Wonder Palace Casino. I tell my Annie not to worry, that it's going to be okay and to remember to lock my bedroom door.

The nurse removes all of my nail polish but doesn't put on anymore. She'll lock up my diamond ring. They push my bed into a faraway room and Mighty Mouse walks beside me. It's the before-they-put-me-to-sleep room. The nurse puts a needle in my arm and shows me a package that looks like frozen soup. It's blood. Mine is too runny and the blood they are using costs lots of money. Don't look at me. I'm not paying.

Mary Mighty Mouse is drinking a coffee and the smell makes me sick. She gets rid of it and asks me about the trips Annie and I have gone on. I tell her that when we were in Florida the staff rented a van and got stuck in the sand and someone told me I look like Anne Murray.

"After we go to the Wonder Palace, I want to go on a plane and fly away somewhere again with my roommate Annie Banana," I say.

There are too many doctors standing around my bed. They are all wearing green hats and coats. The crazy fool who wants me to do number two in a bag tells me they are going to do their very best and that I am in good hands. They don't know what they will find until they take a look.

Mary Mighty Mouse blows me a kiss. Doesn't the staff know this isn't a train station? I don't want her to leave and I don't want to go into the next room.

Before they put a mask on my face, I say to the doctors, "You can't fool me. I know you can die and not know it."

Smother the Others

The air conditioner in the living room window was a house warming present from my new boyfriend. It was a unit Douglas had found at Goodwill on Jarvis; he promised it would be a more effective cooling system after he tinkered with it a bit.

It had been Doug's idea to place my new Ikea king-sized bed in the living room. Often, there were night dwellers who congregated outside the bedroom window doing whatever they wanted to do. No one would be disturbed by sounds of sex through the living room window that faced a fenced-in courtyard.

The blankets were thrown off and I looked at his very manly feet and toes. I wondered if I would pay sometime down the road for making the first move on Doug. We had gone out for three months and at the end of each evening he would shake my hand and say, "Goodnight, Marie."

Finally, I said to him," Doug, I'm attracted to you."

He said, "It's happening alright."

Unlike my former boyfriend, Doug does not try to bewitch and bewilder with words.

I put my arm around his shoulder and kissed him.

Doug mentioned that, although he had changed his shirt that night, he was not a meticulous guy and needed to take a shower.

Doug was released from four years of celibacy, which he'd kept in the hope his ex-wife would give him another chance.

Afterwards he said, "Marie, we're hot."

I agreed.

It seemed inappropriate for me to deliver a talk on sex and responsibility after having initiated the encounter.

We had spent every night together since then. My apartment was larger than his room in south Rosedale.

Doug sometimes talked in his sleep and he also had revealing conversations with himself when he was awake and in the shower.

That morning, while he slept in the dusty, hot room, Doug said, "Crossing guards dressed in black."

The disjointed words were said with a terrified, slurred voice. I touched his shoulder and said, "Wake up, Doug. You're having a nightmare."

In the same, almost automated voice he said, "Doug's not here." He wasn't. Doug was asleep.

Doug's Fender Jazz Bass stood on its stand in the only immaculate corner of the room. Dust bunnies were under my wing chair and mahogany dresser and I noticed a cobweb hanging from the ceiling. Cleaning and vacuuming were impossible to think of on such a sweltering day.

The nightmare seemed to have passed and, even though Doug was still asleep, he had an erection. The thoughts of dust left my mind when Doug woke up and said, "Sex."

"God, it's so sticky and humid, Doug. Wait and I'll fill a bowl with ice and put it beside the bed."

While we made love without a bowl of ice nearby the phone rang. The audio call display read in an electronic voice, "Warrender, Glynn." With my new boyfriend lost in passion, I wondered how the telephone recognized my former lover's name. Glynn would not appreciate a machine associating his name with his cell phone number.

I imagined that Glynn was a third party sitting on the bed. Doug and I were each dripping with sweat and I imagined Glynn was mocking our earthy, traditional lovemaking.

As I was coming, I remembered I had keyed Glynn's number into the phone.

My twelve years with Glynn had been a maze of delicate, surprising deceits. Even during times when he lived with me, I felt like the Other Woman. With Douglas, I intended to be the only woman of record.

Doug was driving his two kids to summer camp and needed to get on the road. He was a devoted separated dad.

"What are you up today, Marie?"

I rolled on my side, turned my back to him, and said, "I'm meeting Glynn. For coffee. Remember Glynn? He's the guy I was involved with for a long time."

"But I'm the best boyfriend you've ever had, isn't that right, Marie?"

For some reason, I started to laugh. Doug was a steady guy, but lacked a sense of humour.

"Glynn owes me some money and he just got an Ontario Arts Council grant."

Doug picked his shorts off the floor and was getting dressed for the day.

"Good for him. Money to sit around all day and do nothing. That's what I want to do with my music. If I get back in time, you and I will have a night out."

On the previous evening, we had browsed at Home Depot and then we went for fish and chips at Duckworth's. Even though my preference would have been dinner and a movie, I was convinced that anyone who spends Friday night at a huge hardware store is a monogamous man. Doug was also the kind of man who would get out of his car to argue with a driver who had cut him off. This tendency made me reluctant to get into his van.

Wearing a white Goodyear baseball cap, a pair of shorts, and a t-shirt from the dollar store, Doug walked towards the apartment door. I felt a twinge of guilt. I had just told my first lie to my new boyfriend. Glynn no longer owed me a penny, but I hoped he would give me some money.

"So, have you mentioned to your ex-wife that you are seeing me?"

"No. It's so busy with the boys when I see her. We never have an adult conversation. Don't worry about it."

I knew I would not rest until the former Mrs. Doug Ferguson knew that the father of her two sons was in love with me.

There were more daunting dust balls in the hallway. After I drank a coffee lying on our bed, I took a shower and considered how I would approach Glynn.

For a year after we broke up, Glynn had given me half of anything he made. Even though sometimes he only made fifty bucks.

During our last six months together, I had supported him. He is a poet, worthy of not working. Neither he nor I kept a record of our financial exchanges. After Glynn moved out last summer to be with the waitress/occasional actor, we made a game of the repayment plan. Glynn would pretend he was paying me for sex. The last payment had been made a month before I went out with Doug.

It was time to make the call. This time I would need to ask for money on the dubious recommendation of my word.

"Glynn, I considered telling you my tooth is about to abscess. I know you're a sucker for a girl in pain. I'm broke and fear my telephone will be cut off. I hate to ask, but can you lend me, say, five hundred dollars until payday?"

"What about your guy? Can't he lend you money?"

"I'm more comfortable asking you."

"I bet you are. No problem, Marie. I'm flush"

"I'll pay you back."

"Sure you will," he said.

We agreed to meet at his bank on Broadview south of the Danforth. I considered riding my bicycle to meet him. Glynn wondered what the attraction was, why anyone would ride a bicycle in the city. I recalled the summer before when, on a Sunday afternoon, I rode along the bike path to the Beaches. It had been as busy as driving in rush hour on the Don Valley. Later, Glynn told me that the waitress he was seeing had also ridden her bike on the same path that day. At the time I had felt violated knowing I had shared the path with someone Glynn was sleeping with. The association had tainted my relationship with my blue Specialized bike.

I walked from my apartment to meet Glynn. Along the way, I drank three bottles of water and took a break at Riverdale Farm. The horses looked miserable standing in their corral. I felt a sense of failure because I could not afford to live in a place with central air or to rescue a horse from the heat.

Glynn was already at the teller. I thought of his balls, his unusually large testicles, inside his black jeans, pressing against the seam of his black, ripped jeans. My new boyfriend did not wear underwear either.

The heavy, scuffed Doc Marten boots he had on were destined for the garbage. He had bought them while he was seeing the waitress, who had influenced his style. They had lasted longer than she had in his life.

He kissed me lightly on the lips.

"I hate to ask you for this money."

"A few months ago I would have given you five grand. Five hundred is a deal."

"God, you look so hot. How can you stand the heat wearing black jeans? Do yourself a favour and buy a pair of shorts."

I ran my tongue over my upper teeth to create saliva.

"I need to get my hair cut. You want me to look like a mook? Why not suggest I wear a baseball cap too?"

"My life is a sea of baseball caps, Glynn. Oh my God, it's fucking freezing in here."

"Would you please shut up about the air-conditioning? Do you have any underwear on?"

"Never during a heat wave."

"That's my girl."

I decided to let his comment slide and took the five hundred dollars he handed me.

"Look, I don't want to be a prick about this. You'll have to pay me back," he said.

"What if I show you my ass? Just joking."

At forty-two, fifteen pounds overweight, it was wonderful to act as though he might take me seriously.

"How much time do you have?"

I marvelled at the freedom of not being afraid of his response.

"Don't get all weird and shit. I don't know why you would. You've got a boyfriend. A woman I haven't seen for twenty years tracked me down. I'm meeting her after we have lunch."

"Were you involved?"

"Briefly, but I was attached at the time. She's an honest woman."

"To have an honest thing with you, she would have to be a detective. I am single." He ran his hands through his thick hair and blew on his bangs.

"You'll fuck her," I said.

"I'm not everyone's cup of tea, you know."

Without discussing where we were going for lunch, we walked towards the Omonia restaurant. For a long time, some things had been predictable with Glynn and me. I suspected he was waiting for me to suggest an air-conditioned establishment but with him I wanted to have dinner on the outdoor patio.

Glynn said, "You are acquiescing without a tiff."

"Just shaking things up a bit," I said.

The waiter recognized us, and I wondered if he remembered the last time we had been there. The memory of Glynn's anger over my finding the poems he had written to the waitress in his knapsack while he was in the washroom had put a damper on the day.

While I was mulling over our last dismal chicken souvlaki meal together, Glynn reached into his pocket and took out a fountain pen.

"This is for you. I thought you'd like it."

"Thanks. It's a Waterman and it is beautiful. It's blue, just like my bike. You must be pissed off at the person who gave it to you. But I'll keep it. I can't believe it – a present from Glynn."

"Don't wound me. I've given you lots of presents," he said. Then he asked, "How's it going with your new man? Have you met his kids? What about his ex-wife?"

I reached into my water glass and took a couple of ice cubes out. I sucked on them, hoping to avoid the question. I knew that Glynn would interpret Doug's reluctance to introduce me to his family as keeping me under wraps.

He said, "Listen, I think my sister might have met your new boyfriend. He played bass for Hogtown Hell Hounds, right?"

"Things used to get pretty incestuous with us, knowing people from the same circles and all. So shut up."

"It was years ago. And she's my sister."

"Well, it wouldn't surprise me if they had met. The artistic community is so small in Toronto. But Doug hasn't supported himself as a musician for about ten years. He renovates houses. Because he wants to stay in town to spend time with his kids."

"'The artistic community.' Aren't you the pretentious little twit now that you've had a letter published in Now?"

"How do you mean 'met'?"

"You know that my sister used to be a stripper. She was working at a bar in Kitchener. The Hogtown Hellhounds played there. Who named that band? It's terrible. The guy she met was married. She said he talked about his wife a lot. She was some sort of pilot."

"The mother of his kids was a bush pilot. About one hundred years ago. He's been divorced for a few years. It could be him. But I doubt it. What are the chances?"

"That's it. A bush pilot," he said.

I reached into Glynn's water glass and took out a few ice cubes, wrapped them in a serviette and rubbed my forehead.

"Doug sees a lot of his ex-wife because they do a lot together with their kids. Of course, I've met all of them."

"Went to Wonderland with the family did you? You're lucky you aren't my girlfriend anymore. How can you do that in public? Wash your face in the bathroom if you have to."

"I'm trying to cool off. Glynn, we had sex in an alley at noon beside a building at Avenue Road and University and this embarrasses you? Give me a break."

He laughed.

I took the fountain pen from the table, took the cap off, and drew a heart on Glynn's forearm.

"Hey, stop. Are you trying to brand me?"

"My relationship with Doug has a proper name. He's my boyfriend. We are becoming a couple. With you, there was never really a word to describe what we had."

"Where the fuck is our food? I have to scramble."

I reminded Doug that the last time we were at the Omonia, I had to pick up the cheque. I told him I had taken his dinner home and ate it the next night.

"A gentleman should pay today is that what you're saying?"

"Hold out your arm Glynn." I was surprised that he did not protest. Inside of the heart I wrote, 'Smother the others.'

Our lunch arrived with some extra pieces of garlic toast.

"Marie, I have to get out of here. My hair appointment is in half an hour. Eat in haste."

"I'm sorry about the crack I made about presents."

"That's right. Do you still wear the diamond earrings I gave you? I kept the book on Alistair Crowley that you gave me."

"What diamond earrings? You gave me a book about Philip K. Dick, a pair of gloves, and a teapot. When I unpacked at my new place, I noticed the bride and groom figurines on the teapot you gave me for Christmas the second time we lived together. If you and I had gotten married, I would've worn a tea cup on my head. With sugar cubes and teaspoon attached to the saucer. I would have glued the cup to a headband," I said.

"I spent a fortune at Northbound Leather, too. What happened to all that stuff?" he asked.

"I kept the corset. But everything else I sold at Doc's Leather on Parliament. I didn't get much, but it helped with closure."

"How can I get this off my arm, you clever little thing. Diamond earrings are my stock present. Some guys give flowers. I give diamond earrings and I can't believe I didn't give them to you," he said.

"Not even when were in the Diamond District."

"We were in New York on your nickel and you told me you hate diamonds. Look, I'm going to be late for Susan. I want to get a haircut before I meet her. Haven't been able to afford one."

"Who's Susan? Right. Your old friend who tracked you down. Not an easy task finding you. Who did you buy earrings for?" I asked.

"Anyone of record." he said.

"The dancer, the waitress, and your two ex-wives?"

"Yes." Glynn smiled with one side of his mouth.

"You're joking, right?"

"I just gave you five hundred bucks and a second ago I paid for lunch."

We left the restaurant and Glynn stood at the curb waiting to hail a cab.

"Glynn, I don't care if you're late, I have a fucking right to a pair of diamond earrings."

"Now you're with a guy with a big working class dick. Let him buy you earrings."

"Did your sister tell you that?"

"Don't be cruel, Marie. She said he was a little arrogant. But that was a long time ago."

"It wasn't him she met," I said. "We don't have a lot of time. There's a little jewellery store just east of here. Chop chop."

"Can't this wait?"

An empty cab was driving west on the Danforth and Glynn raised his arm.

"Okay. You're right. But just not now."

"Absolutely not. It should have happened years ago. You bought fucking Angie earrings. Tomorrow you'll be out shopping for the woman you're meeting tonight."

"You said Angie's name. You didn't call her the waitress."

Glynn put down his arm and I linked my arm in his hoping we would walk by an establishment that sold diamond earrings.

"How far is this store?" he asked.

With every confidence that, in spite of gentrification, the values of the Greek neighbourhood would translate into many jewellery stores within two blocks, I said, "I haven't met Glynn's kids or his ex-wife but I will when the time is right."

"Thought he was a sheep, but he's a wolf. If this place is after Pape, I'm fucking off." he said.

Just before Gough Avenue, I noticed a small store that looked as though it had been there since the nineteenth century.

"I bet you thought I was taking you on a wild goose chase. But here it is, The Limeneria Jewellery Store."

The sales clerk was a woman who seemed to be in her seventies. She was dressed in black. In the way that one imagines a widow might dress.

Most items under the glass had a red tag attached. I explained that I was allergic to cheap metals. I opted to be guided by price and chose a tiny pair of diamond earrings with eighteen karat gold stems. They were not on sale and cost five hundred dollars.

The woman was eager and approached us as though we were in love.

While Glynn paid for the earrings, I said, "You don't need to wrap them. I'm going to wear them."

I put the earrings on, held my hair back, looked in the mirror on the counter and said, "Thanks, Glynn. You didn't have to do this."

He said, "Fuck you. I have to go"

The woman's smile disappeared and I felt we had ruined her day. Glynn hailed a cab.

"Kiss me quick," Glynn said.

He reached around my waist and put his hands on my ass and squeezed.

The Rock

I wanted to meet interesting strangers and never return to Saint Columba. My plan was to finish high school, then travel to England and take the Magic Bus to Istanbul. Instead, I enrolled at the Sudbury Regional Nursing School. The director, Sister Saint Basil, told me to watch my step. She'd accepted me into the school only because my mother's cousin once taught there.

In class we learned about microorganisms on sheets, how to polish our white nursing shoes, and how to give a bath without looking at a man's genitals. Most of the girls who lived in the residence were from small towns in Northern Ontario, and for many of us the pubs at Laurentian University were the best part of living in Sudbury. Sister Saint Basil told us that the twelve o'clock curfew was for our protection. The housemother was a kind woman with a tendency to drink and she did not enforce the rule.

The first week of school, I met Klaus, who'd given up driving a cab in Montreal to study philosophy at Laurentian. He was ten years older than me and thought it sweet that I pretended he was my first lover. He was my second. The housemother turned a blind eye but knew that most nights I missed the curfew.

My mother wrote to tell me that Father Roche from Killaloe had died. When I was fourteen, I told Father Roche in confession that sometimes my stepfather put his greasy fingers inside me. The hardest part was telling the priest that even though sometimes I liked how it felt, I dreamed of murdering my stepfather with a knife. I was relieved that my secret was buried with Father Roche in his early grave.

After Christmas, I stuck a needle in a woman's ass and, with a trembling hand, removed a few sutures from a frightened patient's eye. In the spring, Klaus and I went smelt fishing on Manitoulin Island and he told me he planned to work in Montreal for the summer. A month later, he gave me a kiss and said that we'd meet again in September.

Tim was in Business at Ryerson and he came to Sudbury to work in the mines until the fall. We parked in his MG on our third date and Tim forgave me for not being a virgin. As fall approached, it seemed that Tim and I had a future. I liked it that he saw me as the kind of girl who'd wait until her wedding night, but I missed talking with Klaus.

On the ward, I looked after a biker with a broken leg who gave me a drink of vodka and orange juice out of his water jug. I pulled the curtain around the bed and we drank some more. The next morning, Sister St. Basil had a talk with me and said that I was not suited to the profession of nursing. I wept because I'd failed at something I did not want.

I got a job waitressing at a coffee shop and moved into a pink wooden house with four other people. A guy who lived in the house sold drugs for a living. Before Tim's first visit, I dropped some acid and laughed at him when he walked in through the front door. This was too much for Tim to forgive and he walked out of my life.

There was always a crowd at the house and one morning a stranger stood at the foot of my bed with a shotgun in his hand. As it turned out, he was just joking around. Klaus came back, and to celebrate he dropped some acid. I drank a bottle of gin and we went to see *Straw Dogs*. After the movie, he looked at me and sadly and said, "You used to be so sweet."

I hitchhiked to the pink wooden house and fucked a guy who

drove a pickup truck. Two months later, I took the morning-after pill and was angry that the guy with the truck had not told me his last name. I hoped it was a false alarm and ignored the baby growing inside me.

When my friends at the pink wooden house noticed that I was pregnant, they planned a shower for me and promised to help out when the little tyke came along. To nourish the baby, I ate smelts with poached eggs and passed the time drinking draft at the Coulson. It'd been months since I'd contacted my family and they had not yet heard the news.

In the basement of the pink wooden house, there was an enormous rock that covered half of the floor. The night before my labour started, I'd taken eleven tabs of mescaline and drunk a bottle of wine. I went to the basement to be alone and lay on the rock with a washcloth clenched between my teeth and prayed that my labour pains would go away. When my waters broke, I smashed an empty bottle of tequila against the wall, then went upstairs, stole some money from a guy who was passed out on the floor, and took a cab to the hospital.

The doctor told me nothing about the dead baby and I was afraid to ask how long I'd been pregnant. My guess is that I was about six months when I miscarried. I told the doctor that nature found a way to abort my baby. He thought there was a guy who'd fucked me around and told me to next time find someone with a sense of humour. Some of my friends from nursing school worked on the floor. I discharged myself from the hospital and took a bus to Saint Columba to visit my great aunts, Hanoraha and Peony Devine, at their farm in the Ottawa Valley.

By the time I arrived at their limestone house, my tits were as big and hard as bowling balls. Hanoraha and Peony were pleased to see that I'd gotten fat in the face. There was little to say, so I told them about the rock in the basement of the pink wooden house. My great aunts asked what mass did I get to in Sudbury and showed me their new electric stove.

They made blood pudding, mashed potatoes and beans for supper on the old wood stove. Hanoraha's sons had gone into town to play cards for the evening. Her boys worked the dairy farm and seemed to have few pleasures in life. I thought of these two men who'd shared a room for most of their lives. I vomited in the kitchen sink. I excused myself and took a bath.

The familiar smell of wintergreen in the bathroom terrified me. I lay in the tub and wondered if the baby had been ugly. Hanoraha let herself into the bathroom and in her hands she had pieces of some sheet and safety pins. She leaned her seventy-five-year-old body over the tub and bound my frozen tits. As she was leaving she told me to shave under my arms. When I was six Hanoraha had told me I was built like an elephant, but not to worry because my sturdy feet would get me through life. I wanted her to believe that her predication was right.

In the kitchen, Peony served me a cup of tea, and white cake with maple icing.

She talked about Ewart Pink, the man she was engaged to for thirty years. He came to a sad end on a blustery winter morning when he tried to catch his top hat as it blew over the Mary Street bridge onto the frozen Muskrat River. Peony never played piano again, and slept with Ewart's fiddle in her bed for months after he died. For the first time, I asked Peony why she and Ewart Pink did not marry. Peony told me she did not want to live under the same roof with Ewart, who she said lived in hope and died in despair.

Peony read my tea leaves and saw a man in my cup who was either dead or dead drunk. Milk squirted out of my nipples and left two wet spots on my shirt. Peony told me I should be careful not to lose my head over a man and Hanoraha pointed towards my chest. I told them that I'd fallen in love with a priest whose name was Father Cooper. They both smiled, and Peony told me there was no need to spend the rest of my days saying the rosary from midnight until dawn.

In the guest room, Hanoraha bound my breasts again and told

me to stay at the farm until all of the milk was gone. As a young woman, Hanoraha had married and then came back to the farm with her two sons when her husband tried to kill her with a knife. A year later, she had her daughter and it was rumoured that she'd had an affair with Mick Turner, who trained circus horses and travelled with Barnum and Bailey. As she wrapped the cloth around my chest, Hanoraha told me that her husband tried to kill her when he found her in Mick Turner's arms.

That night, I dreamt about baby skeletons impaled on sticks in a cobblestone road. Their mouths were wide open as though they died screaming. I wept for the dead baby that I despised and wept that it had not known its father. I thought of Flash, the stunning white horse that Mick Turner boarded at the farm when I was young. Hanoraha would send my cousins and me out to catch Flash, knowing that we'd never bring him in from the fields.

I did not return to the pink wooden house, and eventually I travelled on the Magic Bus from London to Istanbul. Afterwards I again visited Hanoraha and Peony at their farm in Saint Columba. I told them that Father Cooper was killed in a car accident on Highway 69 near Sudbury. They believed me when I told them that his ghost said goodbye to them at the British Museum in London.

Peony recalled the drunk or dead man in my teacup. That part of my life had come to a bittersweet end, and it was time to take another peek at the leaves. This time she saw a horse that reminded her of Flash, who once belonged to Mick Turner. Peony did not see one good provider in my cup and she was alarmed that it would not be my good fortune to meet a hardworking man like my stepfather.

Hanoraha told me to thank God for my priest and to hold my head high.

Angel Cake
(*Kathleen Whelan & Sabrina Shannon*)

"It was a bad day. First the tornado, the power went out, and then there wasn't any sweet-and-sour sauce for my chicken nuggets." Words uttered by my niece, Celina, a few years before resonated with me that week.

First, the man I loved took an acting job in the UK, then I found out I had early stage breast cancer, and then I was told that the cat I was to look after in a friend's home near Gramercy Park in New York had died of cancer. I was most upset about the cat and having to perhaps cancel my trip to Manhattan in the fall. Radiation treatments were to start in mid-October at the Cross Clinic at Sunnybrook Hospital.

Celina, who had turned thirteen at the end of May, had come to stay with me from her home in eastern Ontario to attend drama school at SAB Theatre for Young People for three weeks. This was her third year in the program. The theatre was within walking distance of my apartment.

The previous summer she had given me a Beanie Baby – a donkey which she noticed on my computer table when her mom dropped her off. She asked. "Where did you get him?"

"You gave him to me."

"I miss him," said Celina. She went to her suitcase to retrieve a stuffed animal and said, "You can have Babe instead because he's from your favorite movie. My Beanie Babies are an investment and you took the tag off the donkey," she said.

When she visits, Celina sleeps in the bedroom and I use the sofa couch in the living room.

"Can we switch?" she asked. "I want to use the computer at night."

We struck a deal. She would sleep in the bedroom but use the PC whenever she wanted to. That night I deleted my history, particularly any references to cancer, death and dying.

One of Celina's recent presents from her mother had been a fondue set which she had packed in her steamship-sized suitcase filled with art supplies, books, CDs to play on her Walkman, clothes and lip gloss. Eight tubes of lip gloss.

She placed the fondue on the blanket box, which I used as a coffee table, lit the candle and melted the chocolate while I cleaned the strawberries. While we dipped the berries in the milk and peanut-free chocolate, Celina said, "While I'm in Toronto, I want to have fondue all the time."

"Where's your epi-pen?" I asked.

"Can't you see? I'm wearing it. This chocolate is fine. I read the labels and my mother buys it all the time. Actually she packed the chocolate for me." 'Actually' was Celina's most recent over-used word.

A tattered copy of The Saint Columba Cookbook lay on the couch. Celina flipped the well-used pages – well used by my mother – opened her mouth as if she was in shock and said, "Gross. Do they sell calf's feet at the market? We should make this for the kids at drama school."

Beef Jelly for Invalids: Three small onions, three carrots, one small teaspoon of sugar, one ham, a pound of hamburger, and two calf's feet.

When Celina laughed her eyes would get wider. I loved that blue-eyed girl.

"And hasten a heart attack or a stroke in thirteen-year-olds. The first community cookbook was put together by some Northern Irish women to raise money for soldiers after the civil war. These books tell a story. I like to read cookbooks when I can't sleep. That book was compiled by your great aunt to raise money to increase the size of the cemetery."

Celina's laugh was gleeful, confidant and certain.

"This isn't a book. You should read *Harry Potter, Johnny the Homicidal Maniac* or a book by V.C. Andrews. Do you want Heaven when I am finished? Fuck, this cookbook is disgusting."

I wondered how my sister would want me to respond. "Save that language for the schoolyard, Celina. Never swear in front of adults."

Celina made an exaggerated "I am bored look" and said, "Remember when you gave me that book about kids who wrote to a prime minister to save some horses. Where's your boyfriend?"

"He's moved back to England. Diefenbaker, they wrote to him to save the horses on Sable Island."

Celina turned the pages and said, "Can you make this for me? 'Three- to Four-egg Angel Cake.' Just use my margarine instead of butter."

"Look at the name, Celina. It's your grandmother's recipe. The last time I made an angel cake it was as flat as a pancake. We'll give it a go before you leave."

"Granny calls me her little angel, but she has never made me an angel cake."

"Flat as a pancake, too," I said.

Celina was annoyed that her mother had not allowed her to fly on her own from Ottawa to Toronto. During the drive, she had written a story which she offered to show me.

"During the drive to Toronto, I listened to music and wrote a story. Not for fan fiction. Just for fun. It isn't finished yet. Want to hear it anyway?"

"My pleasure," I said.

"Aunt Isabella, you are too nice and too polite."

She stood in the living room, laughed and said, "Pretend you are listening to the radio. "It's called, 'A Girl Named Bob and a Boy Named Kate'."

Her mother had been a hippie at the time. She was also a hater against all those men who thought they were better than women and thought of women as "sex toys."

When she found out she was pregnant, her mother had only been fifteen and so had her boyfriend. Her boyfriend's name was Joe. Her mother had loved Joe very much and he had loved her very much even when he found out about her being pregnant.

Her mother had started to go into labour when attending one of her WAS clubs. WAS was a group her mother had formed that still existed to this very day. WAS stood for Women Against Sexists.

All the women had started to squeal with excitement and they all ran into the car all of them fighting to get in. You see, her mother was very popular at the time and still was. Anyway, the four lucky girls were Lucy, Terry, Stephanie and Amanda.

They were bonded that day. Not in that way, but spiritually. Her mother had formed a friendship after giving birth to her daughter. When her daughter finally came out, her mother held her in her arms looking at her lovingly.

Then she looked over all the women from WAS and decided her daughter was going to be no girly-girl.

"What would you like to name her?" asked the nurse.

"Bob," answered the mother looking down at her baby.

"Bob?" repeated the nurse wondering if she had heard correctly.

"Yes," nodded the mother. "Bob is correct."

"Are you sure? Bob is a boy's name," said the nurse.

"I want Bob. She is my daughter and if I want to name her Bob, darn tooting I will name her Bob!"

The nurse scurried away.

The girls from WAS gathered around the new mother, all gazing at the little baby in her arms.

"She's beautiful, Charlotte," cried Amanda.

A month later, Terry like Charlotte, gave birth to a baby boy. She wanted to look cool in WAS so she named her baby boy Kate. The two of them, Charlotte and Terry, soon became best friends and the leaders of WAS.

Their two kids grew up together. Kate was a little boy with brown eyes and straight hair with long bangs and...

Celina laughed. "And I don't know what happens yet."

"Sounds like creative nonfiction to me, Bob."

"It's all fiction, silly. But my mom is against sexists."

Two years before, on a ski trip to Moonstone, Celina asked me if men could have babies. I told her they could adopt. She said, "Oh no. I heard on Judge Judy that they can." She also told me she knew I hadn't "done it" because I didn't have any kids. On that trip she had told me she would not ski with me because, as she said, "You suck." Celina was growing up.

Celina told me that she told the kids at drama school she was from a weird family which she considered cool. A girl whose parents were "hippies," and did not own a TV agreed with her. Celina was in awe of a girl who had claimed to have given a "hand job." One of the boys had a driver who took him to school and lived on the Bridle Path. She joked if she had a driver she would have her driver sing Spice Girl songs as loud as he could with the windows down. Hannah, who was her best friend and whom she had known for three years, invited her and her mother to her bat mitzvah in November. Hannah also had allergies – Celina looked forward to feasting at a social event, and not needing to bring her own food.

There was a boy, Malcolm, who she had a crush on.

She told me he was a "sex god."

Most evenings we ate at home and then went swimming at the nearby community centre or for a walk to stroll among the one hundred thousand pilgrims who were in the city for World Youth Day. Celina found it exciting because so many were from exotic places. She met many of them during that week.

Twenty girls from the Yukon – each wearing a Catholic Youth knapsack – were sleeping on the floor of a school gym. Their energy was contagious. Celina told them she attended a Catholic school but intended to become a Buddhist and that she was teaching herself how to speak Japanese.

One evening she said she wanted to relax because she had been writing and in rehearsals all day. We rented *Run Lola Run* and *West Side Story*, which had been recommended to her by the director of the drama school. We made popcorn with olive oil, ate Lay's chips and drank Coke.

Drawing anime figures was one of her passions and some of the kids at school had asked her to teach them to draw like her. In the spirit of giving back to the world and pride in her talents, Celina spent her lunch hours conducting drawing classes.

Celina said, "Why do you have a bandage on your boob?"

The moment I had not wanted to deal with was before me.

"I had a lumpectomy. There wasn't actually a lump. Something called calcification. It had to be gone. But I will be fine."

"Cancer?"

"Just a little bit. The doctor told me I won't die from it."

"Are you afraid, frightened or terrified?"

"I was scared when I heard the doctor say the word cancer but relieved when I was told it isn't serious."

"When I almost died, the time I ate the toast, I was too almost dead," Celina said. "Heard my mother yelling at me to come back." She laughed. "I always listen to my mother. My heart stopped because my throat closed."

A new baker at the bakery had added dry skim milk to the mix to make five loaves of spelt flour bread to fill a long standing order made by Celina's mother. The bakery had been making special milk-free bread for Celina for five years.

"Are you ever afraid?"

"No. Because I know what to do. It'll help me to say no to drugs, too."

"How do you mean?"

"I mean that I know how to say 'No'."

Celina insisted on going to see Frank, an Italian stylist who was involved in native spirituality, to have her hair cut when she visited Toronto. She said that Frank and she thought alike. In fact, she would only allow Frank to cut her hair.

This year she requested blonde streaks in her auburn hair. I overheard Celina say to Frank, "We have to call Macbeth 'the Scottish play' or else bad things will happen at our performance. There are so many teenagers from all over the world visiting Toronto. It's so cool. When my mom finishes her master's, we are going to move here. Next summer at drama school I am going to be part of the touring group. We will go to places like Kitchener to put on our play. I can hardly wait."

I wondered what she would eat when she was on the road, in Kitchener, Japan or Berlin, which was the city she had decided she wanted to travel to after Tokyo after she turned sixteen, but I believed Celina would figure it out.

Celina and I were stopped by two travelers from Paris, France who asked her where they could shop, and she directed them to Winners.

At Far Away Farm at Centre Island where Celina had once chased peacocks, we sat with four teenagers from Italy, and at the Science Centre we met a group who were here from Argentina.

Celina was over the moon.

On the ferry returning from Centre Island, Celina struck up a conversation with three enthusiastic youth from Winnipeg. She told them about the time she ate the toast.

"Did you see Jesus?"

"Jesus is dead." She laughed.

With the money her mother had given her, Celina bought a miniskirt at Old Navy and a blue t-shirt with a butterfly in the centre. I allowed her to shop on her own while I waited in lower food court in the north end of the Eaton's Centre.

I read Against Nature, which had been a present from the actor who was not returning to Canada.

Over the internet, Celina had located the store where she was most likely to find the anime DVDs she was looking for. It was at the Atrium on Bay. The clerk, who was about eighteen, was startled when we walked into the store, and he said, "You really look like Drew Barrymore." Although she was much younger than the actress, I realized he was right. They engaged in a lengthy discussion about graphic novels and anime. The movies were available and I purchased them as a summer present for her. She told him she posted a story on a Beyblades fan fiction site. The story was called "Kidnapping Bryan" and had seventy-five reviews and each was rave.

When we were on the subway, Celina said, "Who's Drew Barrymore?" Then she said, "You wouldn't like the story I told him about. Actually, it's too dark and too long for you."

A remake of *Charlie's Angels* was playing in theatres with Drew Barrymore in the cast. Later that night she emailed Malcolm, the boy she liked at drama, to ask if he wanted to go to the movies with her. Malcolm accepted her invitation. Celina said Malcolm looked like Harry Potter and was a "shy sex god."

The actor called from London to say he was not coming back to Canada. I said I had always known we were only playing at being in love.

When Celina was in the fourth grade, she told me she hated her allergies and asthma. I told her that I am allergic to alcohol and had not had a drink for twenty years; since then, when we were at social functions such as a wedding, she had gone out of her way to buy me a Coke and would say, "This is because you can't have a beer like the other adults."

One evening, when we swam in the general swimming area, Celina started a chat with a man who was about my age. She asked him if he would like to swim with us and he smiled and swam away.

She said, "I know you are sad."

Over the weekend, Celina and I had an argument when she wanted to buy a three-hundred-dollar boxed set of anime DVDs. She cried as though she had lost her mother. She said to me, "Why are you saying no all of a sudden?"

Final arrangements were made for Celina to meet the boy she liked from theatre school at Silver City to see Charlie's Angels. Over the telephone she told him that she had had a hissy fit with her aunt because she couldn't get her own way.

Malcolm was very thin and was about a foot shorter than Celina. He had dark-rimmed glasses and seemed every inch a shy boy. She had chosen well. Malcolm had not eaten anything with dairy or peanuts in preparation for a kiss. During the movie, I finished reading Against Nature in the lobby of the theatre.

When Celina and I returned to my apartment, I promised to buy the boxed set for Christmas. Celina said, "First my hissy fit, then the kiss and now this. Actually it's been an awesome day."

The play at SAB Theatre for Young People was scheduled for the same night as *The Way of the Cross* that was to take place in the downtown area.

At St. Lawrence Market, we bought an angel cake pan.

Three to four egg whites, cream of tartar, baking soda, butter, sugar, flour and a dash of salt.

"The play is about teenage stuff like suicide, Aunt Isabella. And you like boring stuff. I hope it doesn't upset you. It's called *Tissues and the Issues that Rip Through Them*."

"Why do you think everyone is so excited about the Pope's visit?"

"Actually, the Pope gives us hope," she said. "But this cake is fucked, Aunt Isabella."

I chose to ignore the language used by my once adoring niece. "If we eat it while it is still warm, it'll be great," I said.

In the art book, one of many, she had drawn five scantily clad anime angels who were floating in front of the sun. In an air bubble one of the angels said, "Beacons of hope like her mother." Celina understood colour. At the bottom of the drawing there was a cartoon drawing —not anime — of a little girl who in cartoon fashion said, "I can't do this without help. If you want me to get it done, you have to help me do it, Angels."

The presentation of the play was more professional than any of the anxious adults had anticipated. As Celina had told her mother and me before the show, "It was a collaborative effort."

Celina played a scowling drug addict, a girl who takes on bullies, and delivered a stellar performance as a teen asking a boy she likes to go to the movies, in hopes of having her first goodnight kiss.

We had forgotten to turn on the video recorder, but there would always be next year.

After the show, her mom gave Celina a gift card to a bookshop on the Danforth and I reminded her of my promise to buy her a three-hundred-dollar boxed set of anime DVDs for Christmas.

With an exaggerated thank you, Celina rolled her eyes.

"Instead, can you buy a boxed set of AC/DC? And I will make copies for my boyfriend, Malcolm. We're going to visit each other and I want to come back at Thanksgiving."

"Not a good weekend for me."

"You said 'no,' again."

When I did buy the DVDs I gave them to Malcolm. He offered copies of his emails from Celina. I thanked him but knew Celina would be pissed off.

We met at the food court at Don Mills Plaza.

She would be furious if she knew she died from an allergic reaction, three weeks after she started the eighth grade.

A psychic told her mother Celina is helping the Virgin Mary bring other dead children into heaven. News of Celina's busy afterlife did relieve my sister's longing for her daughter.

There are things I will tell you when I am dead.

Acknowledgments

Thank you to the Canada Council and the Toronto Arts Council for funding that bought me time to work on this collection. With gratitude to Artscape Gibraltar Point, The Saskatchewan Writer's Guild Writers/Artists Colonies and the Banff Centre's Wired Writing Studio, with a special thanks to Fred Stenson.

An acknowledgment of Tom Walmsley's early encouragement of my work.

A heartfelt thank you to courageous artists Betsy Rosenwald, Mari-Lou Rowley and Mary Walters for your friendship and support.

Thanks to Mary and Tisha Shea for laptops and tea.

I am most grateful to Elizabeth Philips, for her fine editing of this collection and her patience.

Painting and book cover designed by my dear friend David Bateman.

BENEATH US by Giovanni Malito, published with permission from his family.

A BOY NAMED KATE and A GIRL NAMED BOB included in ANGEL CAKE used with permission from Sabrina Shannon's (1990-2003) mother.

Previously Published Works

– Bareback, Kathleen Whelan, subTerrain (Anvil Press) (1999)
– Elvis was Dead, Kathleen Whelan, Other Voices (2000)
– Energy, Kathleen Whelan, Blood and Aphorisms (2002)
– Geography, Kathleen Whelan, Other Voices (1998)
– Smother the Others, Kathleen Whelan, Taddle Creek (2005)
– The Rock, Kathleen Whelan, Other Voices (1994)

Bio Notes about the Author:

Kathleen Whelan's short fiction has appeared in various Canadian journals such as BLOOD & APHORISMS, BROKEN PENCIL, OTHER VOICES; sub TERRAIN and TADDLE CREEK.

Whelan's poetry has been published in an Irish broadsheet, THE BROBDINGNIAN TIMES.

Kathleen's non-fiction was published in New Zealand's ALLERGY TODAY and Alberta's OTHER VOICES.

Kathleen was a producer of "A NUTTY TALE" for CBC's Outfront and was the narrator of a Barry Lank documentary SABRINA'S LAW, produced by the NATIONAL FILM BOARD and GLOBAL.

A limited edition chapbook of Whelan's short fiction titled SWIMMING ON ICE was published by David Bateman.

Kathleen has been the recipient of emerging writer's grants from the Canada Council and the Toronto Arts Council. She has attended the Banff Centre's Wired Writing Studio.

THINGS I WILL TELL YOU WHEN I AM DEAD is Kathleen Whelan's first book.

She is currently working on a collection of poetry, A NIGHT OUT WITH STEVE.

Kathleen lives in Toronto.